Beyond

Contents :

1. THE JUMBO RUBIK'S PRODUCTION CUBE
2. 6 RUBIK'S HANKIES
3. RUBIK'S CUBE CLONING (RUBIK'S CUBE JAR, TRICK CUBE & 8 MINI CUBES)
4. RUBIK'S MENTAL CUBE AND SHELL
5. CLASSIC SIZED TRICK CUBE
6. 56 RUBIK'S MAGIC CARDS
7. 11 RUBIK'S ESP CARDS
8. RUBIK'S CUBE BOX
9. RUBIK'S TUBE
10. INSTRUCTIONAL VIDEO DOWNLOAD

INSTRUCTIONAL VIDEO DOWNLOAD
Fantasmamagic.com/BeyondtheCube

Amazing, easy-to-perform tricks by Steve Vil. Layout by Jack Tawil, Suji Park, & Jessica Mercado.

CUSTOMER SERVICE - FantasmaToys.com/Canada - customerservice@fantasmatoys.com

TRICKS WITH THE RUBIK'S MENTAL CUBE BOX AND SHELL

TRICKS WITH THE RUBIK'S CUBE BOX

TRICKS WITH THE RUBIK'S TUBE

TRICKS WITH THE RUBIK'S CUBE CLONING

TRICKS WITH THE JUMBO RUBIK'S PRODUCTION CUBE

TRICKS WITH THE RUBIK'S ESP CARDS

TRICKS WITH THE RUBIK'S CARDS

MAGIC WITH EVERYDAY OBJECTS

MENTAL MAGIC

RESTAURANT MAGIC

COIN AND MONEY MAGIC

TRICKS WITH THE RUBIK'S MENTAL CUBE BOX

1. THE INCREDIBLE RUBIK'S CUBE!

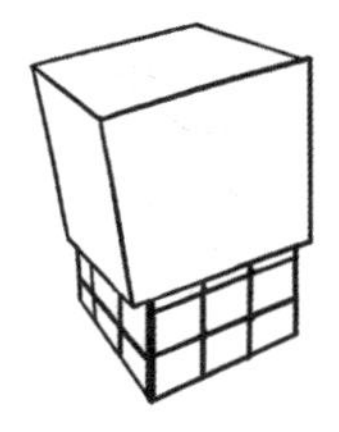

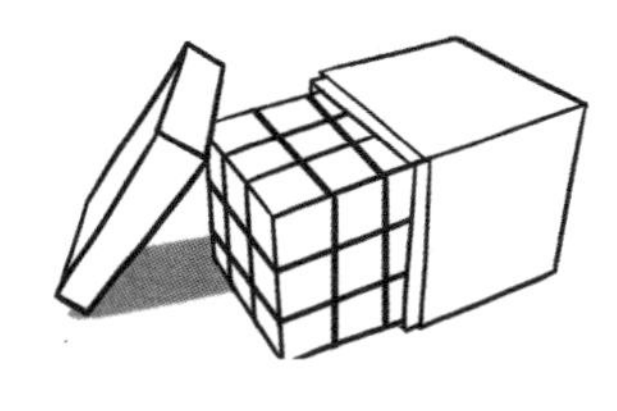

In your set you will find a specially gimmicked Rubik's cube, a shell that looks like a scrambled Rubik's cube and a black box with a lid. Before your show, put the scrambled cube shell over the special cube and place it on the table so the scrambled shell is facing your audience. To your spectators, it will look like a scrambled Rubik's cube! Pick up the cube and show it, being careful to only show the three "scrambled" sides of the shell — you don't want your audience to see the solved side of the Rubik's cube! Now, take the box and turn it upside-down, pushing it over top of the shell and cube. Turn the box with the opening side slightly toward yourself and cover it with the lid. Now, give the box a quick shake up and down. Remove the lid and tip out the Rubik's cube. The shell will stay stuck inside the box, giving your audience the impression that you've solved a scrambled puzzle cube by simply shaking it up and down!

2. THE RUBIK'S CUBE PREDICTION

That's not all that you can do with your Rubik's cube and box! Your Rubik's cube can do another great trick without the shell! Hand a spectator the cube and the box/lid and tell them to put the cube into the box with any side facing up, put the lid on the box then hand the box to you behind your back. Turn around to face them but keep the box in your hands behind your back. Tell them that you will now try and read their mind. Behind your back, move the lid from the top to the front side of the box. Now, bring the box out making sure that the lid is uppermost and the open side is facing you. You will now be able to just glance at the opening and see what colour they picked. Make believe you are still trying to read their mind before naming the correct colour!

TRICKS WITH THE RUBIK'S CUBE BOX

3. RUBIK'S CUBE BOX!

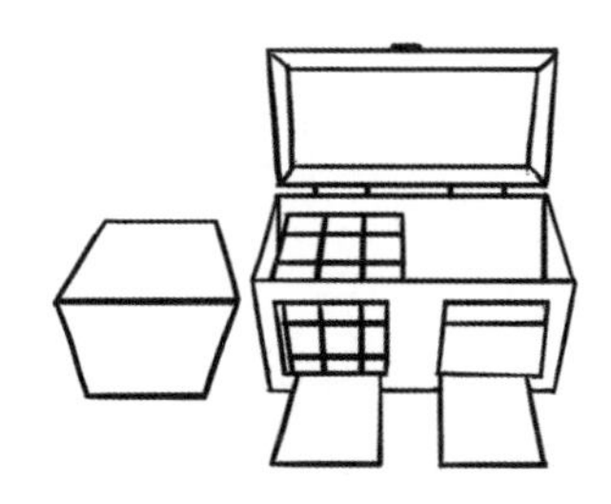

This is a brilliant version of a classic magician's effect used by professionals all over the world! First let's look at the props. You have a box with two doors on the top and two at the front. You also have a three-sided Rubik's Cube shell that will fit snugly over your special Rubik's Cube! You'll also need a cardboard box or perhaps a hat that the cube can fit in to. Show the cube with the shell over it, keeping the shell to the front. Put it into your hat (or box) as you tell your audience that the cube will finally appear in it. Lift out just the shell, leaving the real cube secretly in the hat or box. Make sure to keep the open side of the shell is towards you so that nobody can see that it is not the cube! Now pick up the box with the back facing the audience. Place the shell into the box so that the bottom of the shell is against the bottom of the box and the corners of the shell are in the corners of the box. Now, close all of the doors on the box and claim you have caused the cube to vanish from the box. Prove this by tipping the box so that the cube apparently slides to the lower end of the box then, keeping the box tilted, open the upper front door saying that the cube is gone. Your friends will say that it is at the other end of course! Close the doors and tip the box the other way once again opening the upper front door. Your friends will think that the cube is just sliding back and forth in the box and demand that you open both doors. Open the upper top and front door saying that both doors are open! They will scream for you to open all four doors which you do, proving that the cube has really gone! Now reach into your hat (or box) and remove the real cube to the amazement of all!

TRICKS WITH THE RUBIK'S TUBE

4. THE RUBIK'S TUBE

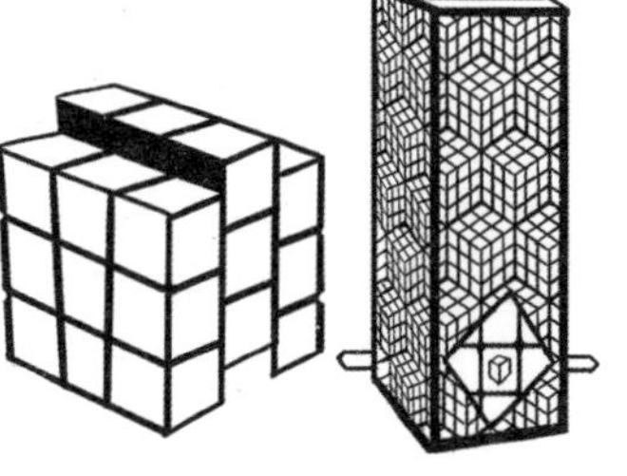

Take a look at your specially gimmicked Rubik's Cube. You will see that it is made up of three separate pieces that are all held together by magnets. Once the pieces are put together, it will appear you have a solid, ordinary Rubik's Cube. You can even twist the sides! You will also find a long tube with windows on the front and back and holes on either side and a small plastic rod in your set. Together, these props make an incredible penetration trick! During your show, show the cube as ordinary by twisting the sides. Don't go overboard, though — you don't want to spend so much time proving the cube is ordinary that you make your audience suspicious: just twist it a couple of times and set it down. Next, pick up the tube and show it empty. Push the rod through the holes in the sides of the tube and tell your audience that the cube cannot fall all the way to the bottom of the tube because the rod is in the way. Prove this by picking up the cube and dropping it into the tube but be sure to drop it so that Rubik's logo on the cube is facing to the FRONT of the tube. If you drop the cube into the tube this way, it will simply hit the rod with a solid, "clunk" and stay there. Now, tip the tube over and dump the cube back onto your work surface. Wave your hand over the cube and tell your audience you've "separated the molecules" of the cube and that it will now penetrate through the rod! This time, drop the cube into the tube with the Rubik's logo facing to the SIDE (even with the rod) of the tube. The centre piece of the cube will hit the rod while the front and back pieces of the cube will drop all the way down to the bottom of the tube! To your audience, it will appear that the cube has penetrated the rod! You can even turn the tube around and show the back window as well! Next, pull the rod out of the centre of the tube. The centre piece will drop down and re-seat itself between the other two pieces and the magnets will pull the whole cube back together. You can now lift the tube up and show the seemingly solid Rubik's Cube sitting on the table!

TRICKS WITH THE RUBIK'S CUBE CLONING

5. RUBIK'S CUBE CLONING

In your set you will find a metal shell that looks like a small Rubik's Cube, 8 smaller multi-coloured cubes and a clear container with a black lid. To set this trick up, you are first going to put the 8 smaller cubes carefully into the bottom of the metal shell. When you set the shell mouth down on the table, it will simply appear to be a small Rubik's Cube. During your show, begin with the shell/cubes set-up on the table as described above. Next, show the clear container and the lid. Pick the shell/cubes up from the table this way: tilt the shell slightly forward and push your thumb underneath the mouth of the shell so the smaller cubes don't fall out. Now, grip the top of the shell with your index finger so the shell/cubes are between your index finger and thumb. You can now show the shell pretty freely from all sides. Next, pick up the clear container and tilt it forward so the mouth of the container is facing the audience. Turn the shell so the opening is facing into the mouth of the container and slide it all the way back to the bottom. Now turn the container mouth-up and put the black lid on top. Next, you are going to give the container an upward shake. When this happens, the shell will stick magnetically to the inside of the lid and remain hidden there, while all of the tiny cubes come showering down into the container! To your audience it will appear the cube has exploded into tiny cubes! Remove the lid and place it mouth-down on the table (so your audience can't see the shell) and dump the tiny cubes out onto the table!

6. CUBE TO BALL

Instead of hiding all of the little cubes inside the shell, you can place other objects inside the shell as well. One good trick is to place a small rubber ball into the shell. When you shake the container up and down, the cube will suddenly transform into a ball that will bounce around inside the container! This can be almost more baffling than Cube Cloning because the cube has transformed in both shape and substance!

7. CUBE TO COINS

Take a stack of small coins and put them inside your cube shell. During your show, ask if anyone knows how much a tiny cube is worth. Before they can answer, shake the container up and down and everyone will be surprised to see it suddenly fill with money! You can't believe how impressive this looks until you try it!

8. CUBE TO DIE

You can take a die (that's singular for "dice") from a board game and put that inside your cube shell. Give it a shake and your friends will be amazed to see a cube turn to a die! If you can manage to gather up two more dice, you can do a great mentalism trick next!

9. MENTAL DICE

Once you've changed your cube into a die, add two more dice for this great mentalism trick! Before your show, write the number "21" on a piece of paper and put it into your pocket. During your show, hand the three dice to a spectator and ask them to roll the dice a few times to prove that they are ordinary dice (they can even use the Cube Cloning container as a dice cup). Now ask the spectator to roll the dice one more time and add up all of the numbers on the top of the dice. Now ask them to add up all the numbers on the bottoms of the dice. This number will ALWAYS be 21! Once they announce their final number, pull out your prediction to show you were correct!

10. THE PSYCHIC CELL PHONE

Before your show have a friend who has access to a cell phone help you out with Mental Dice. Tell your friend that he or she will be getting a phone call asking for The Great Erno and they are to say to the person they will be speaking on the phone with "the total of the dice is 21!" Instead of revealing the number 21, have them call The Great Erno for an amazing revelation! This is an incredible effect that can be done anytime, because once you have let your friend in on the trick then anytime someone calls them asking for The Great Erno they will know what to do!

11. CUBE THROUGH TABLE

This trick is great for when you're seated at a table. Tell your friends that you are going to make your cube (actually, the shell) penetrate through the table. Place the cube on the table and put the clear Cube Cloning container mouth-down over the cube. Now take a piece of newspaper and cover the container with it. Press it down all around the container so the paper holds the shape of it. Now, pat your hand on the top of the container and lift it with the newspaper still around it, up and over your lap. Point out that something must have gone wrong because the cube is still there. While your friends are looking at the cube, secretly let the container slip out of the newspaper and into your lap. Because the newspaper is the same shape as the container, they will not think the container is no longer there! Place the now-empty container back over the cube and smash it again with your hand so the newspaper crumples. Now reach into your lap and pull the container out from under the table saying that you don't know your own strength!

TRICKS WITH THE JUMBO RUBIK'S PRODUCTION CUBE

12. THE JUMBO RUBIK'S PRODUCTION CUBE ILLUSION

Start by unfolding the lid of the box so that it is out and away from the rest of the box. Open the box so that it resembles a cube shape. On the bottom of the box (the opposite side to the lid) you'll see three narrow flaps with hook-and-loop tabs in their corners. Press each tab to its partner tab. This helps the box to keep its square shape. Now reach into the box from the bottom side and pull out and unfold the section that is going to become your load chamber (a secret area where productions will be hidden!). You will need to twist and unfold it — almost turning it inside out. Again you will see two hook-and-loop tabs on the outside of the back wall. Press the load chamber against those two tabs. You will find that it helps to use your other hand to assist by inserting it into the box from the lid side and applying pressure against the back wall. At the bottom end of the load chamber you will see a tab sticking out on each side. Insert these into their respective slots on either side of the load chamber to lock it into place.

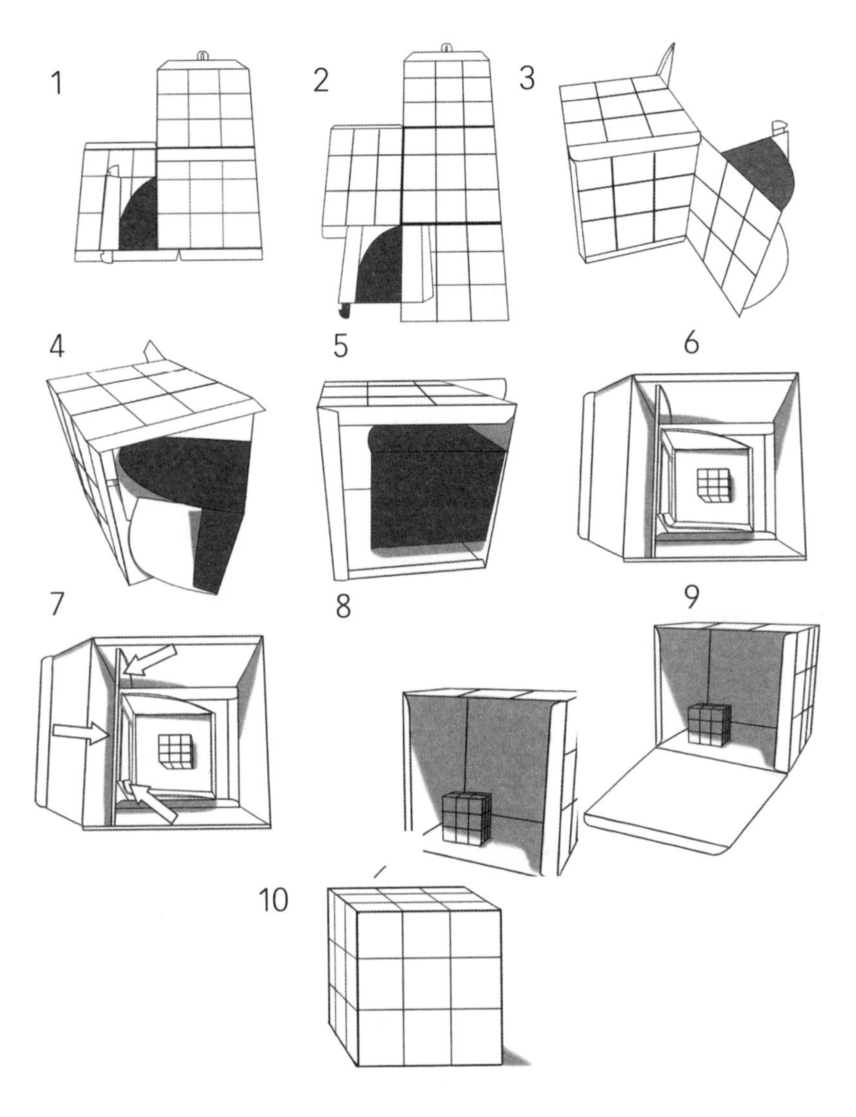

13. HOW TO PERFORM AN INCREDIBLE PRODUCTION!

Before your show, put the special edition cube from your set in it the load chamber. Place the silk handkerchiefs into the box, outside of the load chamber. Have the box facing your friends so that the front is facing them. Tip the box forward (away from you) until the top of the lid is facing your audience. The load chamber remains on the table. Open the lid to reveal the box is empty apart from a few handkerchiefs. You can either remove them or leave them in the box. Close the lid and immediately tip the trunk towards yourself so that the lid is uppermost. Open the lid and show that the handkerchiefs have turned into a real cube!

14. MULTIPLE PRODUCTIONS!

You can make your trunk a running gag through your show to fully exploit its amazing secret. For example you could have all your show props as your production in the hidden chamber. Show the box empty and produce just your first prop. After the effect show the box empty again then produce your second prop! Do this after every effect and the box becomes a great effect for your audiences!

15. A COOL SHOW FINISH

At the end of your show you can then put the props you've used back into the trunk and, for a final extra miracle, everything vanishes to bring the show to a truly magical close!

16. ANOTHER COOL SHOW FINISH!

In your load chamber also have some candy. At the end of your show, for a final production, produce the candy to share with your friends to thank them for watching the show. You'll not only be a great magician but a very popular one too!

17. A LITTER OF LITTER

Set your trunk up to produce a stuffed cat or dog (don't try this with a live animal!) and show it to be empty. Take a paper tissue and claim that, as the world's greatest origami artist you will create a group of baby animals from it. Now shred the napkin and proudly announce, to a huge groan from your audience, that it is now a litter! Throw the pieces into your trunk and produce the stuffed cat or dog from the box as you announce, "And here's the mom!"

18. TORN AND RESTORED

Your production cube can also be used to switch objects provided that they are flat enough to fit into the section between the load tray and the box wall (where you loaded the silk earlier). Get two of the same newspaper page and put one into the load chamber and the other between the load chamber and the wall of the box. During your show open the trunk and remove the newspaper letting the box be seen to be empty. Now tip the trunk back and tear up the newspaper throwing the bits into the box. Wave your hands over the box and remove the second paper to show that you have magically restored it!

19. TORN AND.... RESTORED?

Rip up one of your papers and tape it all together with black tape so that it is very obvious. Have this in your load chamber and a duplicate paper in the front area. During your show open the trunk and remove the paper. Just as you did before rip it up throwing the bits into the trunk. Claim that you will "magically" put the paper back together and toss a roll of tape into the box. Wave your hands over the top and, to a huge laugh, pull out the taped together one. Finish by saying, "Well how else could it be done?"

TRICKS WITH THE RUBIK'S ESP CARDS

20. THE RUBIK'S ESP CARDS

The eleven ESP cards are very unique: you will find one card (the "key" card) featuring nine different colours (Red, Orange, Yellow, Green, Blue, White, Purple, Black and Pink) and ten other cards, each featuring a different configuration of the above colours and a large hole where two of the colours are missing! You can use these cards to read your friend's mind! Begin by showing your friend the key card. Ask him to choose a colour but to not tell you which colour — just to think of it. Next, pick up the other ten cards and one by one show them to him, asking him if his colour appears on the card. Place all of the "yes" cards in one pile and all of the "no" cards in a separate pile. When he is finished, pick up the "yes" pile and place it face-down on the key card. Make sure that this is facing you and not him! When you place the "yes" pile face-down on the key card, the cards will form a window through which only one colour can be seen: that is the chosen colour! Once you've seen and remembered the chosen colour, pick up the "no" pile and place it on top of the "yes" pile on the key card. Now, turn the key card over and announce that you've magically determined the chosen colour even though some of the cards had two colours missing! Announce the colour you saw through the window and blow your friend's mind!

1

2

TRICKS WITH THE RUBIK'S CARDS

21. THE RUBIK'S DECK

Your deck of cards has a special marking system that will allow you to know which card is which just by looking at the backs! There is a key which tells you how the marking system works on the back of this manual but I will offer a quick explanation: each suit is represented by a different colour — blue = Spades, green = Clubs, red = Hearts and orange = Diamonds. Down the left side of each card, you will see a row of yellow squares in groups of three. Depending on where a colour is located in the row, that indicates which card is on the front. For example, if the first square in the yellow row is blue, that indicates the card is the Ace Of Spades. If the blue square is in the second square in the yellow row, that means it's the Two Of Spades. This continues on down the yellow row with the eleventh, twelfth and thirteenth squares indicating the Jack, Queen and King, respectively.

22. IS THIS YOUR CARD?

The easiest way to use the deck is simply to find a chosen card. Although very basic in appearance your clean handling of the deck will convince the helpers that you must have fantastic skill! Have a card chosen and, as your helper looks at it, you remember which card it is by secretly reading the marks on the back of the card! Let them shuffle cards as much as they like then take the deck back from them. Look through the faces of the cards and finally pull out their card and watch their jaws drop!

23. EXTRAORDINARY EYESIGHT

Have a card chosen by your helper and ask them to cover it with their hand. Before they cover it make sure that you have read the secret markings on the back so that you know which card it is! Claim to have the most amazing eyesight in the world and offer to prove it to them. Very quickly riffle through the cards, pretending to note each and every one. The faster you do this the more impressive your trick will be! Finally close up the deck and tell them the card — they'll be convinced that you have the eyes of an eagle!

24. I CAN READ YOUR MIND

This effect is all about your acting ability. Have a card chosen and returned to the deck (making sure that you read the marks on the back!). Now let them shuffle the cards. Ask them to concentrate on their card but don't just tell them what it is. Instead slowly get the colour then the suit and finally the value of the card. Pretend that you are concentrating very hard and they'll really believe that you have uncanny E.S.P. powers!

25. MULTIPLE MIND READING

You can take this a stage further by having three cards chosen. Get two put back into the deck and get your third helper to put their card in one of their pockets. Read the marks on all three cards and remember them! Slowly get the first two cards then pretend that the third card is even harder because it is sitting in their pocket. Of course it isn't any harder than the first two but your acting here convinces them that it must be! The presentation that you use is just as important as the trick! When you get the third card take a deep breath and say, "That was tough!"

26. A WEIRD COINCIDENCE

Split your deck into two halves and give one to your helper. Ask them to take a card from their half and to remember it. Be sure to check out the marks on the back of their card so you know which one it is! Now ask them to push their card in among yours. As you shuffle your cards say, "Since you gave me a card it is only fair that I give one back to you!" Quickly remove their chosen card and hand it to them. Ask for the name of their card and spread your half out onto the table. Their card isn't there! Show that you gave them back the very card that they gave you!

27. MATCHING PAIRS

Take the Ace through Six of Hearts from your deck and give them to your helper to mix them up. As they are doing this you remove the Ace though Six of Spades from the deck and fan them out faces toward yourself. Ask them to put any one of their six cards face down on the table. Concentrate for a moment and secretly read the markings on the card they placed on the table to identify it. If you wish, you can shield your eyes with your hand as if concentrating hard but still get a good peek by looking under your fingers. Put the matching number card on top. Ask them to put another card face down next to the pair and, once more put the matching number card on top. Repeat this until you have six pairs of cards on the table. Then, turn over the pairs to show a perfect match on every one!

28. MATCH ME IF YOU CAN!

Here your helper is going to try and match pairs with you! As well as the marks on the cards you are going to use a very sneaky magician's principle known as the One-Ahead System! Remove the Ace to Six of Hearts and Ace to Six of Spades from the deck just as you did in the previous trick. Put one card down on the table and ask them to put a card on top of it. Now put down the matching card to theirs on top of the pile. Ask them to put another card on top and once more put the matching card to it on top. Continue until all the cards are gone! The last card will be the match to the one on the bottom of the pile (the one you put down first) so you need to make a tiny adjustment. Pick up the pile and hold it in your hand. Take the top card of the pile and say, "I want you to take the cards one at a time and deal them face up in a line onto the table here" Use the card you are holding to point to a spot on the table. Now casually return the card to the pile but replace it on the bottom! Now hand them the pile and they will deal out six perfect pairs proving that they are a mind reader as well!

29. LUCKY MATCHES

When doing the above effect they will sometimes put a perfect match down on your first card. If this does happen put the pair to one side and say, "We'll look at those later, I've got a good feeling about them!" Now carry on as before using your One-Ahead System. At the end turn the first pair and say, "An amazing match but it gets better!" Now, as before ask them to deal the rest of the cards (making your adjustment) in a line to show all perfect matches! Sometimes the second pair may be a perfect match as well! If so, put it to one side as well, saying something like, "This is feeling more than a little spooky!" before continuing. Once in a while you'll get five perfect pairs and, when this happens, play it up as a total miracle!

30. RED AND BLACK

Have your helper shuffle the deck then ask them to put a black card and a red card face up, side by side, on the table. Make the crazy claim that you can feel, from the weight of the ink on them, whether a card is red or black and ask them to hold out one card face down to you. Lightly touch your fingers under the card and, having read the marks, announce which colour it is. Ask them to put it, still face down, onto the face up card of the colour you called. Say, "We'll see just how I did in a few moments!" Go through the whole deck calling the colours and having them put into the appropriate piles. Turn over the two piles to show that you have magically splitthe deck into twenty-six red and twenty-six black cards without any mistakes! You can always read about a dozen each of the colours and stop there if you wish — it is still just as effective!

31. SUIT YOURSELF

Having separated the deck into red and black you can take this one stage further by claiming that not only can you feel red from black but can also tell the suits apart! Have them pick up the red cards and hold them face down. If they want to, you can say, they can shuffle them again if they want. Now repeat the actions of the above effect but this time, using the marks, separate the hearts from the diamonds. Repeat this whole process again with the black cards until you have four piles of cards on the table. Turn them over to show that you have separated out all of the suits!

32. PERFECT PLACEMENT

Have your helper lay out five cards (A, 2, 3, 4, 5 of any suit) in a row face down on your table. Carefully study the cards and say, "Not quite a perfect row but it's pretty close!" Now say to them, "I'm going to turn my back and I want you to swap two cards. I'm willing to bet that you can't make the row look exactly the same!" Turn your back and let them change two cards around. When they've done it turn back and say, "Not a bad try but these are the two you changed, they just weren't quite the same as before!" Of course you are using the secret marks to see which two were changed (just look to see which two are out of order) but they don't know that! You can repeat this over and over with them going berserk trying to position the cards correctly but three or four times is enough. If the order is still the same that means your sneaky friend did not swap any cards and tried to trick you!

33. THE KEY CARD (TOP)

Shuffle your deck of cards and secretly remember the bottom card of the deck. Spread out your cards face down and have any card selected by your helper. Ask them to remember the card as you square up the deck. Ask them to put their card face down on top of the deck then say, "Of course it is a little easy for me to find it there so I'll lose it in the deck!" Give the deck a straight cut and complete the cut. A straight cut means lifting off about half the cards and placing them to one side then putting the remaining cards on top. Ask your helper if they would like to cut the deck as well. As long as they are straight cuts they can cut the deck as many times as they like! Now look through the deck and look for your key card. The chosen card will be the card directly to the right of the key card!

34. THE KEY CARD (BOTTOM)

Shuffle your deck of cards and secretly remember the bottom card of the deck. Spread out your cards face down and have any card selected by your helper. Ask them to remember the card as you square up the deck. Ask them to put their card face down on top of the deck then say, "Of course it is a little easy for me to find it there so I'll lose it in the deck!" Give the deck a straight cut and complete the cut. A straight cut means lifting off about half the cards and placing them to one side then putting the remaining cards on top. Ask your helper if they would like to cut the deck as well. As long as they are straight cuts they can cut the deck as many times as they like! Now look through the deck and look for your key card. The chosen card will be the card directly to the right of the key card!

35. YOU'VE BEEN PRINTED

A great way to use a key card is to have the card chosen and "lost" in the deck. Say, "Unless my detective powers are low I think I'll be able to find your card by looking for fingerprint or DNA evidence upon it. I may also use my amazing powers of smell but perhaps that little more information than was required!" Pretend to search through the cards carefully examining them (perhaps even sniffing one or two of them) before finally saying, "This one has you all over it!" as you reveal the correct card!

36. THE POLICE GET THEIR MAN

Again a key card is used here in a sneaky way. A card is selected and returned to the deck. Now you say you need your "two policemen" and start to look through the deck. Remove the two black Jacks and put them on the table. During this time also look for your key card and cut it to the bottom of the deck (leaving their card on top). Either put the deck under the table or behind your back and pick up the Jacks. Say that you are going to put them face up in the middle of the deck. What you actually do is put one second from the top of the deck then the other one on top (trapping the chosen card between them). Now give the deck a straight cut and bring the deck out again. Spread the deck to show the card between the jacks and have your friend confirm that it is their card!

37. THIS TRICK TAKES A YEAR, A MONTH AND A WEEK

Turn the bottom card of your deck face up. Have a card chosen but be careful that they don't see the reversed card. Have the chosen card replaced on top of the deck then cut the cards. Spread through the cards and 'notice' the reversed card. Cut it to the top and turn it face down. The chosen card is now second from the top just where you want it! Ask them how many weeks there are in a year. When they reply fifty-two, deal - one card at a time - five cards in a pile and then two cards in a pile next to it. Put the two cards on top of the five then put all the cards back on the deck. Ask how many months there are in a year and, when they say twelve, deal twelve cards - one at a time - into a pile on the table. Once more put them back on top of the deck. Finally ask how many days there are in a week and, after the reply, deal seven cards in a pile and replace them on the deck. Now, turn over the top card of the deck and reveal their chosen card!

38. LOST

Another great way to use your key card location is to make them think that you may just have messed up the trick. Have a card selected and, as before "lost" in the deck. Say, "I'm going to deal the cards one at a time into a face up pile and see if I can magically find your card!" Start to deal the cards and look for your key card. When you see it you know that the very next card will be their card but don't stop dealing. Deal a few cards past their card then say, "The very next card that I turn over will be your card!" They've seen their card already dealt so they think you have made a mistake! You prove them wrong by reaching into the dealt cards and pulling out their card!

39. LISTEN TO MY VOICE

This is a fun way to use your key card location. Have a card selected and 'lost' in the deck. Say, "Let's play a game to see how good at controlling your voice you are!" Give them the deck say you'll turn your back to them. They are to deal the cards one at a time face up onto the table naming them as they do so. You claim that you'll be able to tell, just from their voice, when they get to their card! Of course all you do is wait till you hear your key card and you know the next one is theirs!

40. SCANNER

Start with the four aces on top of the face down deck and hand it to a spectator. Ask them to deal cards one at a time into a pile onto the table and to stop whenever they like. Ask them to deal more than ten cards at least though to make it harder for you. Once they have stopped dealing ask them to pick up the dealt cards and to deal them into four piles one card at a time. When they have finished say, "I couldn't know how you would deal so how do you explain this?" Ask them to turn to top card of each pile and there, amazingly, are the four aces!

41. REPLICAS

Remove the four Kings, four Queens, four Jacks and four Aces from your deck. Lay out the four Aces in a square and on top of each ace place a King. On top of the kings place a Queen followed by a Jack. Gather the piles together and turn them face down. Give your pile a few straight cuts then deal out four new piles one card at a time. Now turn your four piles face-up to show that in one pile are the four Aces, in the next the four Kings and so on!

42. ACES TO THE TOP

Before your show remove the four Aces from the deck and put them into your pocket. During your performance get a helper to shuffle the cards as much as they like. Take the deck from them and put it into your pocket on top of the Aces already there. Reach into your pocket and remove the Aces one at a time to show your incredible skill!

43. THE DOUBLE-BACKED CARD

Begin with the double-backed card on top of the deck. Spread the cards in your hands to show that all of the cards are face-down. Now explain that this is a very stubborn deck and that any card that is turned face-up in the deck will automatically turn itself face-down! Ask a spectator to take the top card (the double-backed card) but to not turn it over. Now, turn the deck over and re-spread it so all of the cards are face-up and tell the spectator to put the card anywhere in the deck that he wants. Now, close the deck and turn it over again. Respread the deck and show that none of the cards are face-up: his card has stubbornly turned itself face-down again!

44. SUPER DOUBLE-BACKED CARD

You can make a big feature of this effect by having a number of cards selected! You can use ten to fifteen chosen cards but three should be enough for you to start with. Do the effect exactly as above but this time replace all the chosen cards in different places. Square the cards up and say, "One card is tough but finding three would be a miracle!" After going behind your back and turning over the bottom card put the deck face down on the table and say, "Not only did I find them all but I put them back in face up in less than three seconds! Spread the deck to show that you have done it and your applause will be sensational!

45. STUBBORN DECK

Begin with the double-backed card on top of the deck. Spread the cards in your hands to show that all of the cards are face-down. Now explain that this is a very stubborn deck and that any card that is turned face-up in the deck will automatically turn itself face-down! Ask a spectator to take the top card (the double-backed card) but to not turn it over. Now, turn the deck over and re-spread it so all of the cards are face-up and tell the spectator to put the card anywhere in the deck that he wants. Now, close the deck and turn it over again. Respread the deck and show that none of the cards are face-up: his card has stubbornly turned itself face-down again!

46. CARD THROUGH HANDKERCHIEF

Have a spectator choose a card and place their chosen card back on top of the deck. Next, with the deck in your left hand, cover the deck with a handkerchief. Reach underneath and remove the entire deck from your hand leaving the top card (the chosen card) in your left hand. Place the deck on top of the handkerchief in your left hand, directly over the top card hidden underneath it. Now, fold the part of the handkerchief closest to you forward and over the deck. You will be able to see the edge of the hidden card facing you. Now, fold the rest of the handkerchief down and around both the deck and the hidden card. You will see that the deck is completely enclosed in the handkerchief but that the chosen card is able to come out of the bottom of the handkerchief! Pick the handkerchief up from the top, allowing the deck to hang beneath it. The chosen card will stay inside the folds! Reach up into the folds and slowly pull the chosen card out. Now, hand the handkerchief and deck out for examination so your spectators can see that the deck really is wrapped in the handkerchief!

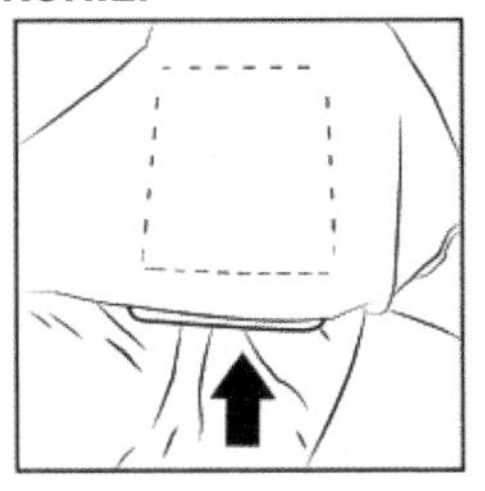

47.ONE WAY OR ANOTHER

Some decks of cards have a "one way" back: in other words, they have one picture rather than a symmetrical design. Your deck has a special design by this because the yellow stripe only goes down the left side of the cards! Begin by making sure all of the backs are facing in the same direction. During your show, spread the cards face-down and have a spectator choose a card. Square the deck up then turn it around so the opposite end is facing the spectator and have them put their card back. Now, spread the deck with the backs facing you and you will immediately be able to tell which card is the chosen card: it's the card that's upside-down!

48. TWO CARD MONTE

Take a look at your two special cards. One is a double-faced card and the other is a double-backed card. The audience is not supposed to know that these cards are trick cards! Put the double-faced card on top of the double-backed card. Have the top card (double-faced) angled toward the right so you can see the bottom card too, just like a fan of cards. Hold the cards gently between your thumb on the top card and your first finger on the bottom card, towards the centre of the cards. Show the cards to your friend by holding them as instructed and then turn your wrist over at the same time as you slide the top card to the left. When your wrist is turned, they will now see the other side of the double-faced card, believing it to be the second card. Then turn your wrist back and again slide the top card, this time to the right. Practice this turning motion, to get it right, so it doesn't look like you are doing anything sneaky. Then take the top card (double-faced) show it to your friend and put it behind your back as you ask your friend what card that leaves in your hand. They will of course say the name of the other card. With your hand still behind your back, simply turn the card over and then bring it out with the other side showing, proving them wrong!

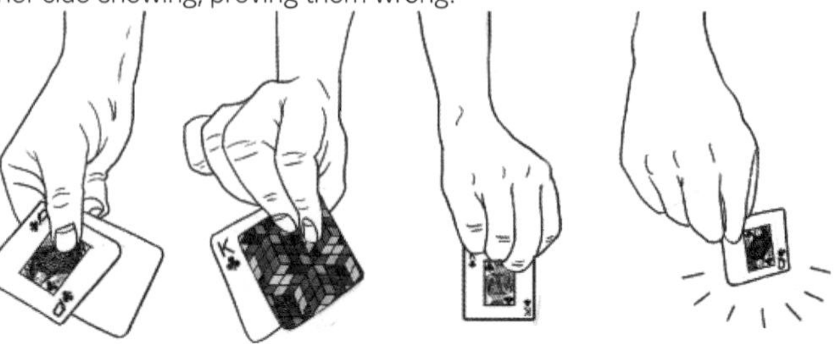

49. THE JOKER

You will notice that one of your Joker cards has a monkey staring into a mirror. There is a card in the mirror. If you force the card that's in the mirror, you can use the Joker card to reveal the force! A good way to do this is to force a card (two easy card forces are below) and shuffle their chosen card back into the deck. Tell the spectator you will find their chosen card and remove the joker. Of course they will say the Joker isn't their card.... Until you ask them to take a closer look at what's in the mirror!

50. CROSS CUT FORCE

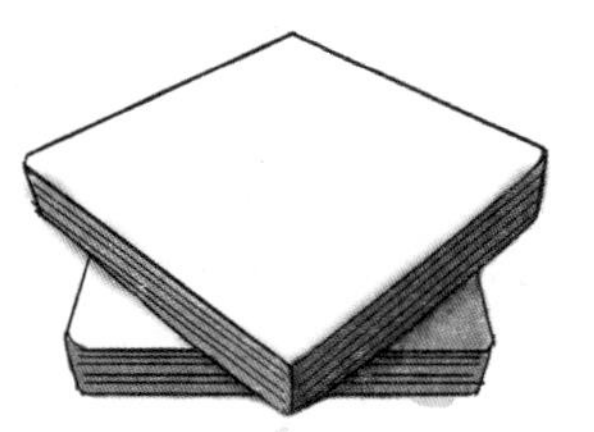

Before your show, place the card you want to force on top of the deck of cards. Now ask your helper to cut the top half of the deck to one side. Pick up the lower portion of the deck and put it diagonally on the cut off cards. Now, briefly distract them by saying something like, "you could have cut the deck anywhere" or "the choice of where you cut the deck was entirely yours, yes?" Now lift off the top portion and ask them to take the top card of the lower portion. This is the force card!

51. THE 10/20 FORCE

Before your show, put the card you wish to force 9th from the top of the deck. Now ask a spectator to name a number between 10 and 20. Ask them to hold the deck and to count one card at a time into a pile on the table until they have dealt the number they named. Then ask them to add the two digits of their number together (so if they named 16 they would add 1 and 6 to get 7). Ask them to deal down to that new number using the dealt off pile of cards on the table. After they have done that, tell them now that they have discarded these cards to the table, the very next card in their hand will be their card! This of course, will be your force card!

52. MIRACLE STOP

Deal out 21 cards face up in three columns of seven cards each, by dealing three across, and then three across again, until each column has seven cards in them. Ask a helper to think of any one of the cards and to point out which column it is in. Square up the columns and put them together making sure that the column with the selected card in it goes in between the other two. Deal out three new columns and ask again which column has the selected card. Gather up the columns again making sure that, once more, the cards with the chosen one in go into the centre of the assembled piles. Repeat this once more by dealing out three new columns and once more making sure that the cards with the chosen one in go in the centre of the other two packets. Now turn the packet face down and spell the words "Miracle Stop," removing one card for each letter. When you turn over the letter 'p' it will be the chosen card!

53. SPELLING BEE

Before your show, take out Ace through 10 of any suit and arrange them in this order (from top to bottom, all facing down): the 3 on the top of the packet, next a 5, next an Ace, then 8, followed by a 10, then 2, 4, 6, 7 and the last card 9. When you are ready to perform, take one card from the top of the packet, as you say "A", then place this card on the bottom of the packet keeping it face down. Then take the next card from the top of the packet and place it on the bottom, as you say "C." Then take the next card from the top and turn it over face up as you "E, and that spells Ace." An Ace will show. Place this Ace on the table. Take the next card from the top of the packet as you say, "T" and place it on the bottom of the packet. Then take the next card from the top as you say "W," and place that card on the bottom of the packet and finally turn the next card from the top over as you say, "O." Now a two will show. Put it on the table and continue counting. Do the same for the numbers three, four, five, and so on until you get to ten which will be the last card in your hand. Turn it face up as you say, "Ten!"

54. PROFESSIONAL SPELLER

Before your show, put your special spelling packet in reverse order from the previous effect: so in this version, the top face down card will be a 9 and the bottom card in this special packet will be a 3. Place this whole packet face down on top of the deck. After the special packet of cards is set and you have memorized the bottom "key" card you are ready to perform this very cool trick. During the show, take out the deck of cards and ask one of your helpers to cut the deck. Then take back the cards and look through the faces for the key card. Immediately under the key card will be the "nine" of your special packet. Split the deck at this point and put the key card and everything above it under the other packet. So you should now have a deck of cards with the key card back on the bottom of the deck and your special packet, still in order on top of the deck. Count off ten cards from the top of the deck face-down to the table. Now pick up the packet and perform the trick as you did before.

55. ROYAL SPELLING BEE

There will be three picture cards in this version to be spelled after the ten. They are the J-A-C-K, the Q-U-E-E-N and at the very end you'll turn over the King! Here is the order from top to bottom: 3, 8, 7, A, Q, 6, 4, 2, J, K, 10, 9,and 5 on the bottom of the face-down packet. Perform this trick the same way you did the previous version, except for one very important twist: you must now spell the value of the card using one card for each letter and then after it has been spelled, you will turn over the very next card to show that it has been spelled correctly.

56. SPELLBOUND

Let's use the key card for a different kind of spelling effect. Have a card chosen and "lost" in the centre of the deck. Now look through the deck pretending to be looking for their card. As soon as you see your key card you know what their card is. Don't say anything but keep sliding the cards over and as you do so, silently spell each card past the chosen one as the card. For example, if the card is the Ace of Clubs, the card behind it (actually your key card) is spelled as A, the next one as C, the next as E until you reach the "S" in clubs. Cut the deck at that point and complete the cut. Ask them to deal cards spelling one letter of their card for each card dealt. They incredibly spell to their card!

57. SPELLDOWN

Before your show, put nine cards to one side. Then, on top of the deck, put the following cards in this order face down (from top to bottom): Two Of Clubs, Six Of Hearts, Four Of Spades, Eight Of Hearts, Jack Of Diamonds and the Eight Of Diamonds. Place the nine cards you put to one side on top of this set up and you are ready to go. Say to a friend, "I'm going to take some random cards from the deck." As you say this casually remove nine cards and put them to one side. Now take the next six cards (your set cards) and spread them out in a fan to show your friend. Ask them to think of any one of the cards. After he has done that, replace them on the deck. Finally put the nine cards on top of all. Ask them to name their card. Spell their card with one card for each letter. It doesn't matter which one they thought of, the final card will always be theirs!

58. GRANDPA'S LETTER

On a piece of paper write, "I knew you'd get into trouble one day so I'll help you out by telling you that the chosen card is the four of clubs! Love from Grandpa." Seal this into an envelope and keep it in your pocket. During your show force the four of clubs on a friend (remember we learned how to do that earlier!) and then ask them to shuffle the deck. Start to look for their card but pretend to be having trouble finding it. Finally say, "There's only one hope folks. A year ago my Grandpa sent me a letter saying it would help out in times of trouble!" Bring out your letter and ask your friend to open and read it aloud. Finish by saying, "Good old gramps, he's the man!"

59. PROFESSIONAL LETTER

If you really want this to be totally convincing address the envelope to yourself and send it through the post. That way it will have a genuine post office stamp upon it. You might also want to crumple it up a little bit to make it look older.After all you are claiming that the letter is a year old so it wouldn't be in perfect condition after that time!

60. INVISIBLE REVERSE

For this trick you will need your marked deck and an normal deck. Reverse the Five Of Hearts (5H) in your normal deck and have it in its card case. Use your marked deck to force a 5H on a friend then say, "I'm going to try to make one card magically turn over in the other deck!" Pretend you are removing an invisible card from the normal deck, turning it over and replacing it. Now really bring out the deck and spread it to show a reversed card! Ask them what card they originally picked and show that your reversed card matches it!

61. X MARKS THE SPOT

On the back of the Ten Of Diamonds (10D) in your normal deck draw a large X. Have this set near the centre of the deck. Force the 10D from your marked deck on a friend then tell them that a trunk of ten diamonds was hidden by a pirate. Tell your friend to look through the other deck until they find the X that marks the spot where the treasure is hidden. They will search through the normal deck and will be astounded to find that the card marked X is their chosen card!

62. THE MISSING CARD

Take the card you plan to force from your normal deck and put it into your pocket before your show. During your show, force your force card using your marked deck then ask them to remove the matching card to their chosen one from the regular deck. Of course they won't be able to because it's missing! Finish by removing it from your pocket and showing you knew ahead of time which card they would choose.

63. CARD TO ORANGE

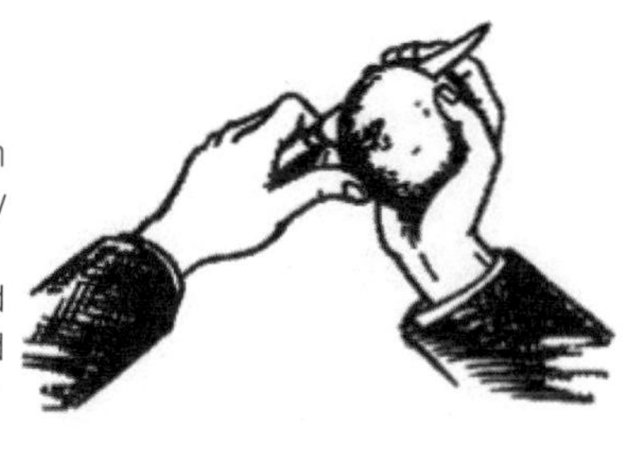

You could put that extra force card anywhere from in your wallet to in a balloon, a bottle or an orange. The vanish of the card from the ordinary deck just makes it seem much stronger. Say you are using an orange. You would force a card from the marked deck and ask them which card they chose. Then say, "I'll try to make that freely chosen card vanish from this other deck and reappear in that orange!" They'll think you are joking around until you show that you can do just that very miracle! Push a pencil into an orange to create a hole through the middle. Be careful not to push the pencil through the other side! Now roll up the force card and push it into the orange. Do this secret preparation before your show! You can now reveal at the end of the effect that their card has been magically transported into the orange by cutting around the outside of the orange and pulling it apart (younger magicians, please get an adult to cut the orange open for you)!

64. PROFESSIONAL CARD TO ORANGE

To really make this look extra special carefully remove the stem from an orange and make your hole there. After pushing your force card into the orange you can now use some rubber cement to glue the stem back into place. Now the orange can be shown freely before opening it!

65. MAGICIAN'S CHOICE

Place an orange in a bowl with an apple and a banana. Now ask a spectator to choose a piece of fruit. If they choose an orange, proceed as normal with the trick. If they choose an apple or banana, put that piece of fruit aside and say, "Okay, we won't use this piece of fruit". Then ask them to choose another piece of fruit. If they choose the orange, proceed with the trick. If they choose the other piece of fruit, put it to the side and say, "now we've eliminated two pieces of the fruit and all that's left is the orange" then use the orange to do your trick. This technique is called, "Magician's Choice" and is a way for the magician to get the audience to choose exactly what he wants them to.

66. CAPPED

Props needed: Someone else's fingers!

Carefully uncap a cola bottle and drink a small amount. Now roll up your force card and push it into the bottle. Using the eraser end of a pencil, flatten out the card inside the bottle as much as you can so that it looks as though it could not have gotten into the bottle. Now recap the bottle. After showing that your force card card has vanished from the other deck, you can bring out the cola bottle and ask somebody to uncap it for you. Pour the cola into a glass and reveal the selected card inside!

67. BOTTOM'S UP

Props needed: Two paper clips and a dollar bill (or a bill-sized piece of paper).

Prior to your show, on the bottom of a soda bottle or any other object write with a marker the words "The Ten Of Hearts." During performance put an ordinary card under the object saying that you will use it later on. Now force the Ten Of Hearts using one of the forcing methods you've learned and have it returned to the deck. Say, "Wouldn't it be amazing if your card was already under here?" Have them lift up the object only to discover it is the wrong card! You then say, "No, I meant actually under the object! Take a look underneath!" They will look at the bottom of the object and be amazed to see the words the "Ten Of Hearts!"

68. DON'T FORGET IT

This is a fun joke to lighten up the show between your other amazing magic tricks. First, have your spectator choose a card and ask them to remember it. You quickly read the mark on the back of the card then return it to the deck. Let's imagine, for example, that they've chosen the Three Of Clubs: as you shuffle the cards, say, "Now don't forget your card, just keep saying the 'Three Of Clubs' over and over again to help you remember it." Of course, you've just named the card that they've chosen!

69. THE ART OF CARDISTRY

Your special marked deck can also be used as an ordinary deck of cards. You can perform many tricks and stunts with it, just as you would with any deck! Below are some tricks and stunts that you can perform that don't require you to use the marking system at all. In fact, you can do these tricks with any deck of cards so if you don't have your marked deck handy, you can borrow any deck and amaze your spectators!

70. THE WATERFALL

The object of this is to drop the cards from your right hand into your left hand so they fall in one continuous stream of cards. It will take some practice but is not as difficult as you think! You're going to start with half of a deck of cards. Begin by holding the deck by the ends between your fingers and thumb and letting them bow backwards slightly toward your palm. Now hold your left hand about four inches (10 cm) below your right hand and release the pressure on the cards so they spring out one at a time and land against the palm of your left hand, resting on your thumb. As you get better at this, you can increase the distance up to a foot (30 cm)!

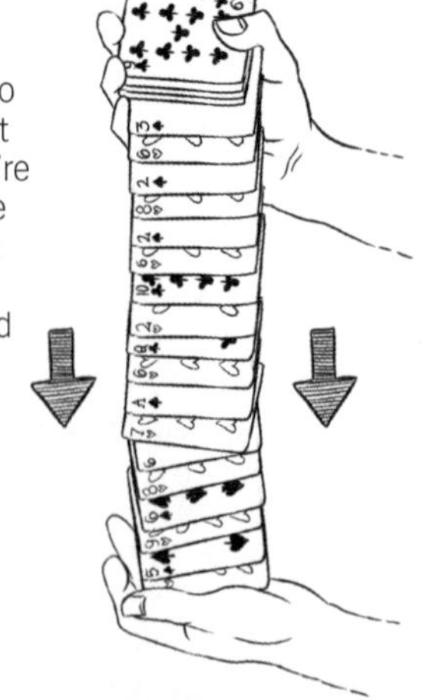

71. SPRING DECK

This is similar to The Waterfall except that instead of using light pressure and gently releasing the cards into your left hand, you are going to increase the pressure and "shoot" the cards from your right hand to your left hand! Begin by setting up a half of a deck as you did in The Waterfall by holding it by the ends and allowing it to bow inward toward your palm. Now, squeeze your fingertips together as you allow the cards to slip out of them and they will shoot from your right hand to your left! Begin with a short distance between your hands (a few inches/cm should do it) and gradually increase the distance as you get better at catching the cards.

72. THE ONE-HANDED CUT

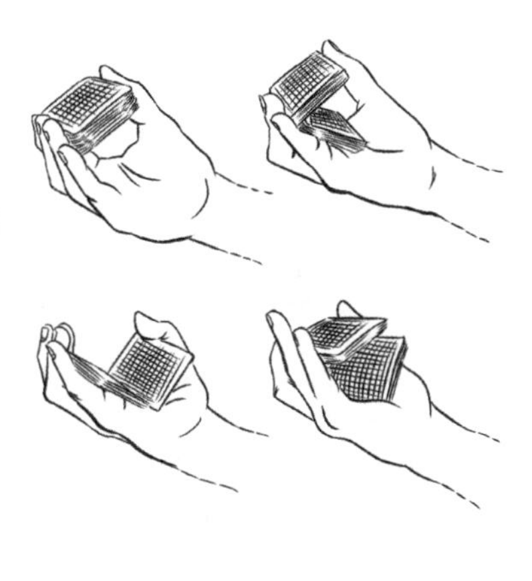

Cutting a deck of cards isn't always an impressive feat but with this method- called The Charlier Pass- you can do it one-handed! Begin by holding a deck above your right palm using only your fingertips. Now, release about half of the deck with your thumb, by moving it upward and pressing it against the uppermost portion of the deck but loosening your grip on the lower part. This will cause half of the deck to fall into your palm. Now, use your index finger to push that half of the deck upward against your thumb: this will make the deck look like a little "tent." Next, allow the top of the deck to fall into your palm as you push what was the bottom of the deck on top of it with your thumb. Square the cards up and you've just performed a one-handed cut!

73. THE CARD SPREAD

First note: it is best not to try to do this on a smooth surface as the cards will slide and not spread evenly. Hold the deck with your thumb on one side and your middle finger on the other. Your index finger will be on top of the deck. On a tablecloth or a card mat, spread the cards in one fast motion while pushing down on the top of the deck with your index finger. Practice this until the cards spread smoothly in a straight line across the table. Now, turn over the card on the bottom of the opposite end and press down on it: the rest of the cards will also turn over in order and the entire deck will flip face-up!

74. HOW TO THROW A PLAYING CARD

Take any ordinary playing card and grip it loosely between your index and middle fingers. Next, curl your fingers and hand inward toward yourself. Finally, quickly thrust your arm forward and straighten it, allowing the card to fly out from between your fingers. Congratulations! You have just thrown a playing card! With a little practice, you can throw cards so fast that you can actually get them to pierce styrofoam or even a piece of fruit!

75. OUT OF CARDS

For this brilliant effect you'll need to make up a special card. Using a permanent marker pen write on one card ,"You have just run out of cards!" Use a bold colour and a small value card (like the two of diamonds) so that the words stand out clearly. Put this card in the 21st position from the top of the deck and you are set to do a miracle! Ask your helper to cut off a small pile of cards from the deck. So long as they take less than twenty-one the trick will work so stress that they don't take too many cards or the effect will go on forever. Ask them to hold their cards behind their back so that you can't see how many they have taken. You now deal twenty-one cards onto your table one at a time into a pile. Don't count out loud but just be casual as if you needed some cards. Pick up your pile and deal one card face up onto the table. The helper then brings out one of their cards. Keep alternating with you then the spectator dealing. When the spectator runs out of cards your very next card will say, "You have just run out of cards!" So long as you follow the instructions the trick will work itself though the helper will give you credit for having uncanny skill!

76. TELEPATHIC CARDS

The magician shows three cards and asks a spectator to think of one of them. He puts the three cards in his pocket. Then he brings out two of the cards and lays them on the table. "'If you have been thinking of your card, it will be the one that is still in my pocket. Tell everyone the name of your card." "The three of clubs," replies the person who is thinking of the card. The magician reaches in his pocket and brings out the three of clubs! In his pocket, the magician has previously hidden two additional cards. When he shows the original three cards and puts them in his pocket, he notices their order. He then reaches into his pocket and brings out the two additional cards and places them on the table. The audience believes that they are two of the three cards he just put in his pocket. When the spectator names the card he is thinking of, the magician just has to bring out the correct one of the three cards that are in his pocket!

77. THE RISING CARD

Here's how to make a card rise from the middle of the deck, as if by magic! Start by removing three cards from a deck of cards. Now, put a rubber band around the deck, from top to bottom (not around the middle- the rubber band should be around the long ends of the deck). Now, you are going to divide the deck in half and open both ends of the deck outward so the rubber band is stretched between the two halves of the deck. Place one of the three cards you previously removed against one half of the deck (and the rubber band) then close the other half on top of it. Hold this very tightly or the rubber band will just pop the card right out! Now, place the two leftover cards on either side of the deck to hide the rubber band. It will look just like a regular deck! Now, place a clip at the top of the deck to hold everything together. During your show, unclip the deck and hold it tightly. Bring out the deck and show it to the audience. Now, wave your hand over the top of the deck and gently release the pressure on the deck. If you do it very carefully, the card will slowly rise out of the deck in an eerie manner!

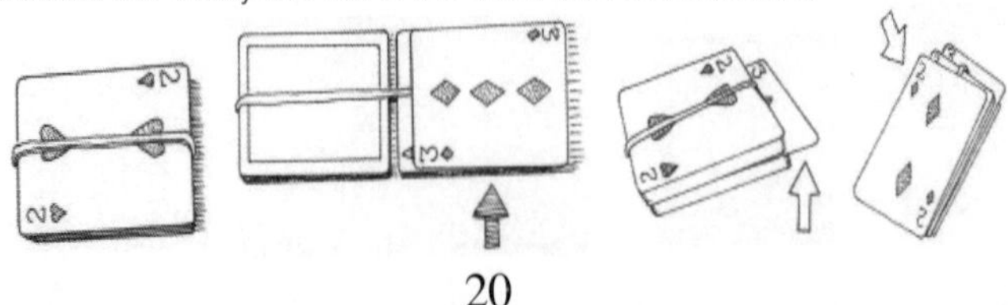

78. POPS RIGHT OUT!

Do all of the above but this time, put all four Aces in the centre of the deck. Now, instead of having the card in the centre rise eerily out of the deck, claim you will make all four Aces jump out of the deck! Release the pressure all at once and the Aces will fly out of the centre of the deck!

79. THE CHOSEN RISING CARD

Begin by cutting a long slit up the centre of the back of a playing card box. The slit should be about the length of the design on the back of the box (not extending into the tab) and about ½ an inch (1.3 cm) wide (if you are too young to use scissors, please have an adult help you). If you place your deck into the box with the card design facing the slit, it won't look like there is a slit there! However, keep that side face-down on the table anyway. During your show, remove the deck from the box and place the box slit-side down on the table. Have a spectator choose a card and return it to the top of the deck. Now, place the deck into the box again so that the top of the deck is facing the slit you made. Leaving the top of the box open, hold it between your fingers and thumb with your index finger at the bottom of the slit. Now, simply slide your index finger up and it will look like the chosen card is rising from the deck!

80. THE SECRET PEEK

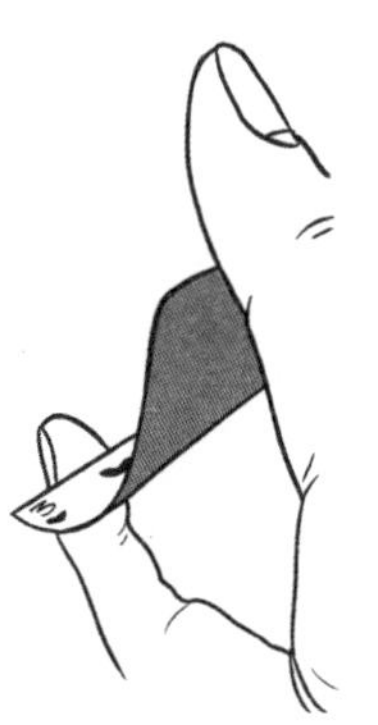

You can tell your audience you have eyes in your fingers! To prove it, you are going to deal the cards off of the top of a deck, face-down, instructing your audience to tell you when to stop. Once they've had you stop on a card, hold the card up, face forward with the back of the card to you. Grip the card by the long ends (i.e. the top and the bottom) with your right hand. Now with your left hand, press your left index finger into the centre of the card. This move will bend the card in toward you slightly and you will be able to see the bottom-left corner of the front of the playing card! Simply say the name of the card and your friends will believe you can really see with your fingers!

81. THE KINGS' DOUBLES

Begin by taking all of the Jacks and Kings out of an ordinary deck of cards. You are going to then do this: pile all of the Jacks on top of your right hand then place a King on top of them. Next, place the last three Kings on top of the first King but in a fan formation. During your show, hold the Jacks and Kings as explained above- it will appear to your audience that you are only holding four Kings. Next, square the cards up and place them face-down on top of the deck. One by one, take all four of the Jacks (which will be the first four cards on top of the deck) and push them at random intervals into the deck. Make sure you do this with all the cards facing down! Snap your fingers and turn the top four cards over, revealing that the Kings have jumped back to the top of the deck! You can now spread the deck and show there are no Kings in the deck other than the ones you removed from the top!

82. THE KINGS' DOUBLES 2

Here's a much simpler version of the above trick for beginning magicians. Remove all four Kings from a matching deck of cards. Now, place all eight Kings (four from the matching deck and four from the deck you are using) on top of the deck. During your show, remove the first four Kings and fan them to show your audience. One by one, push them into the deck. Snap your fingers over the deck and remove the second set of four Kings to show that they have jumped back to the top of the deck! Now, take all four Kings and put them in your pocket. Make another magical pass over the deck and say the Kings have returned to the deck. Spread the deck, face-up, to show the Kings are indeed back in the deck!

83. POINTS SYSTEM

If you look through your deck, you will see that certain cards are "pointers": take for example the Seven of Spades-it has seven pips and five of them point in the same direction. The aces are pointers as well as the threes, fives,sixes, eights and nines. Take all of the "pointers" and arrange them so they point in the same direction then put this packet of "pointers" in the centre of the deck. During your show, spread the deck so that one of these pointers from the middle of the deck will be chosen. While the spectator is memorizing their card, square the cards up and flip the deck around. Have them return their card to the centre of the deck. Spread the cards so that the faces are facing you. You can easily tell which card is the chosen card because the "pointers" will be pointing in the wrong direction!

84. PENCIL MARKS THE SPOT

Using a pencil, draw a thin line on one end of the deck. During your show, spread the cards and have a spectator choose one. While he's looking at his choice, square up the cards and spin the deck around. Have your spectator put his card back into the deck anywhere he chooses. Now, to find his card, all you have to do is look for the pencil mark on the opposite (blank) side of the deck!

85. WELL-SUITED

Another way to find a chosen card is to take all of the cards of one suit (let's say The Hearts, for example) and put them together in the centre of the deck. During your show, have a spectator choose a card from the ends of the deck (NOT the centre!) and then replace it in the centre of the deck. A quick spread of the cards will reveal the chosen card: it's the only card that isn't a heart

86. THE BENT CORNER

In this trick, the magician fans the pack and holds the cards with the faces toward the spectator, inviting him to touch one of the cards. As soon as the spectator does so, the magician's left thumb, which is hidden behind the pack, bends the corner of the selected card upwards. After the pack has been shuffled, a glance at the corner of the pack reveals the position of the chosen card!

87. THE X-RAY FILES

The magician takes a pack of cards from the case and holds the case behind his back while inviting anyone to insert a card, face down, in the case. He closes the flap of the case so that the card will be entirely concealed. The magician then holds the card case to his forehead and instantly names the card that is in the case, although no one has seen it! Before your show, cut a small hole in the lower right corner of the back of the card case. Hold the case back downwards with your thumb always covering the tiny opening. When you raise the case to your forehead, simply move your thumb aside and catch a glimpse of the corner of the card inside the case!

88. THE COLOUR-CHANGING DECK

Separate the red cards from the black and arrange the two portions very carefully, so that every other card is red and every other card black. Push the two sections together but stop before the ends are flush. Put the joker on the bottom of the pack. The result is this: When one end of the pack is riffled, only red cards will be seen. In transferring the cards from one hand to the other, they are turned around and when the other end is riffled, only black cards will appear. Finally, use your fingers push the two sections flush together; so when the cards are riffled the third time, both colours will be seen. You can even hand the deck out for examination!

89. THE ODDS OF EVEN

A pack of cards is divided into two halves. A spectator selects a card from one half and places it in the other half which is shuffled. The magician looks through the half of the pack and immediately discovers the chosen card! In one half of the pack are all the odd cards — ace, three, five, seven, nine, jack, and king. The other half contains the even cards. No one will notice this. When a card is placed from one section to the other, the magician can immediately discover it when he looks through that portion of the pack.

90. EVEN MORE ODD

A spectator deals himself a small packet of cards and the magician also deals himself a small packet."Count your cards," says the magician. "If your total is odd, my cards will make it even. If your total is even, mine will make it odd." The person counts his cards and the magician adds his packet. The spectator's total is immediately changed from odd to even, or from even to odd as the magician predicted! Simply deal yourself an odd number of cards and the trick is sure to work. Odd plus odd will produce even while even plus odd will be odd. Thus you are sure to change his total!

91. A VERY SILLY JOKE

Sometimes it's fun to split up your miracles with a joke or two. This one is very silly indeed. Have three cards chosen and then shuffled back into the deck. You don't need to try to control them at all! Hold the deck and say, "Do you want them one at a time or all at once?" If they reply, "All at once," just throw the entire deck at them! If they reply, "One at a time," start tossing the cards one at a time at them. Either way it's a good laugh!

92. ANOTHER SILLY GAG

Have a card selected and returned to the deck. Now ask your friend to think of the value of their card and add three to it. Then ask them to multiply their new number by two, add five, take away seven and keep going on for ages randomly getting them to do silly math. The longer this goes on the funnier it gets. Finally ask them their total. Think for a second and name any card. Of course you'll be wrong but it's a funny gag!

93. SERIOUSLY SILLY

Actually when doing the above gag you will be right every now and then by chance making it a silly gag with a miracle finish. Sneaky magicians here will have already worked out that you can be right every single time by forcing a card on them at the start of the effect!

MAGIC WITH EVERYDAY OBJECTS

94. I BROKE MY THUMB

Props needed: Your thumbs!

This classic piece of hand magic makes it appear like you break off your thumb and put it back on unharmed! Hold out your left hand with its palm towards you and the thumb on top. Now bend your left thumb in at the joint so that it points to you. Bend your right thumb and put it next to your left thumb with your right first finger covering the line where the thumbs touch. Practice this so you can set the position without anybody seeing what you are doing! From the front it should look just like you have curled your right first finger over your left thumb! Now move your right hand to the right and it will look as though you have removed your thumb. Move it back it looks as though you have replaced it!

95. I BROKE MY FINGER

Props needed: Your fingers!

1. Why stop at your thumb when you can also appear to break off a finger as well! This one will take little more practice to get the illusion just right but the effort is well worth it, as it looks so good! Bring your two hands together with the right first finger going under the left hand and the right second, third and little fingers going on top.
2. Underneath the left hand your right thumb pushes against the right first finger bending it to the right.
3. Two things now happen at once as the hands separate with a snappy motion. First you bend the left first finger inwards and secondly the right second, third and little fingers curl in a little to expose the bent right first finger. The illusion is so astonishing that you may even get a scream or two when you do this!

96. STRETCHING A FINGER

Props needed: Your fingers

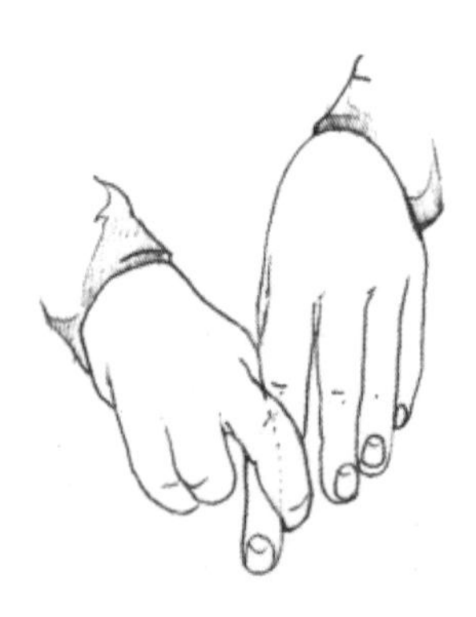

The start position is the same as if you were going to break off your finger (or at least appear to do so!). Instead of pulling your hands apart you place them with the left first finger on top of the right first finger with the left first fingertip hidden under the curled over right first finger. As you work into position grunt as little as you claim to be stretching your finger. When you are in position you can show that your left first finger looks impossibly long. The angles are quite critical for this to be totally convincing so do some practicing before a mirror to get them just right!

97. THE APPEARING HOT DOG

Props needed: Someone else's fingers!

This optical illusion is always a nice one to throw in among your finger effects. Tell your helper that you will conjure up a hot dog in mid-air that only they will be able to see! Get them to hold their hands out about a foot in front of their face and about a foot apart. Now have them point the first finger of each hand tip to tip towards each other as they slowly bring their fingers together and finally allow both tips to touch. Tell them to relax their eyes and try to look at something in the distance as the two fingers come towards each other and finally touch. If you try this yourself you'll see the optical illusion of a tiny hot dog floating between your fingertips!

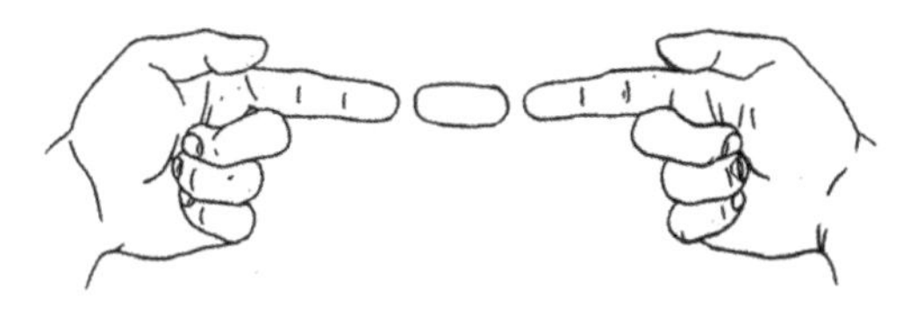

98. THE LINKING PAPER CLIPS

Props needed: Two paper clips and a dollar bill (or a bill-sized piece of paper).

For this wild effect, you'll need two paper clips and a dollar bill. If you don't have a dollar you can use any currency or a piece of paper. Fold the bill into an "S" shape and clip it together, with the open end of the dollar clipped to one side of the inside fold and the other end of the dollar clipped to one side of the other inside fold. Now pull the ends of the paper apart—the two paper clips will fly into the air and link together all by themselves!

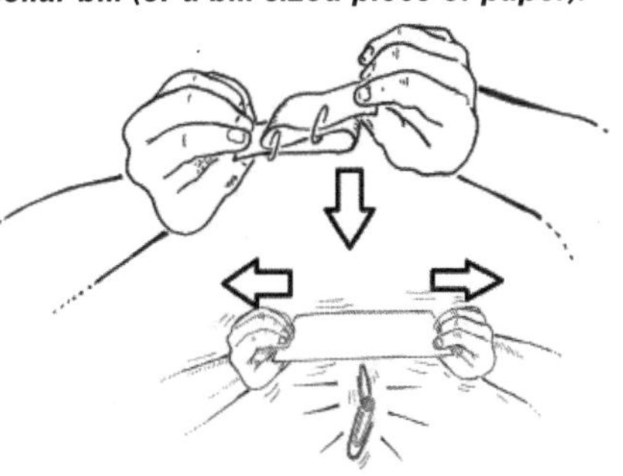

99. SUPER LINKING!

Props needed: two paper clips, a rubber band and a dollar bill

If you add a rubber band to the set-up as shown in the picture, you can create an even more amazing miracle. Clip one side of the dollar as you did before, but before you clip the other side, slip a rubber band onto the open end of the dollar and push it all the way to the folded end, then use the second clip as you did before. If everything is set as shown, take a deep breath and pull on the ends of the paper. The two paper clips will link together—and one of them will link onto the rubber band as well!

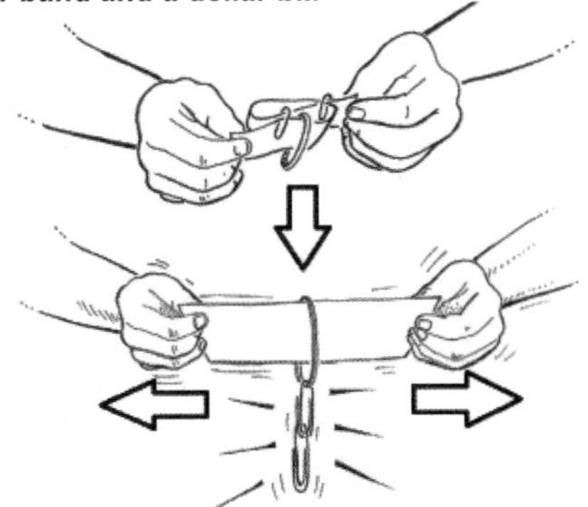

100. THE JUMPING RUBBER BAND

Props needed: A rubber band.

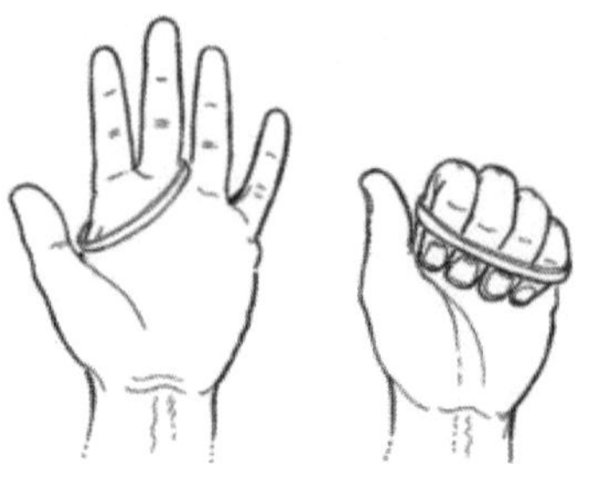

Keep a few rubber bands in your magic hat pocket and you can do even more amazing magic! Put a rubber band over your first and second fingers. Make sure that your palm is facing you and the back of your hand is toward the audience. Curl your fingers down into a fist, but as you do, pull the rubber band out towards you and slip all of your fingers inside of it, letting the rubber band rest against the bottom part of your fingers, near the nail. From the front where your helpers are watching, it will appear as though the band were around just the first two fingers. Say a magic word and straighten your fingers out. The band will magically hop onto your third and little fingers!

101.THE TRAPPED JUMPING RUBBER BAND

Props needed: Two rubber bands.

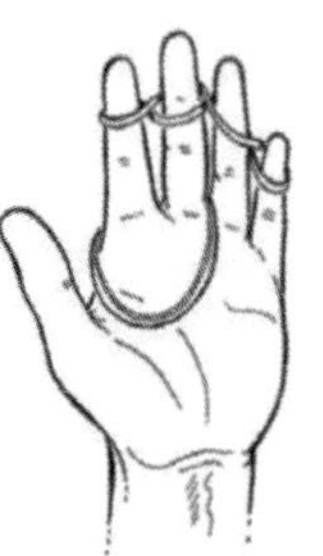

If you twist another rubber band around the tips of your fingers as shown, it will appear as though the first rubber band cannot escape. But, astonishingly, if you perform the moves as you did in the previous effect, the effect will still work!

102. DOUBLE JUMPER

Props needed: Two rubber bands.

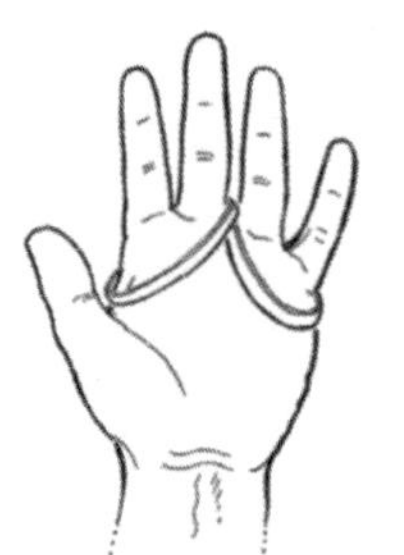

Another great follow-up to the previous tricks involves two different-coloured rubber bands. Put one over your first two fingers and one over your third and little fingers. Close your hand into a fist, fingers towards you, and put all four fingers into both rubber bands. Now, when you straighten out your fingers the rubber bands will change places. This will even work with a third band twisted around your fingertips, as in the trapped rubber band trick!

103. CREEPY

Props needed: A broken rubber band and a borrowed ring.

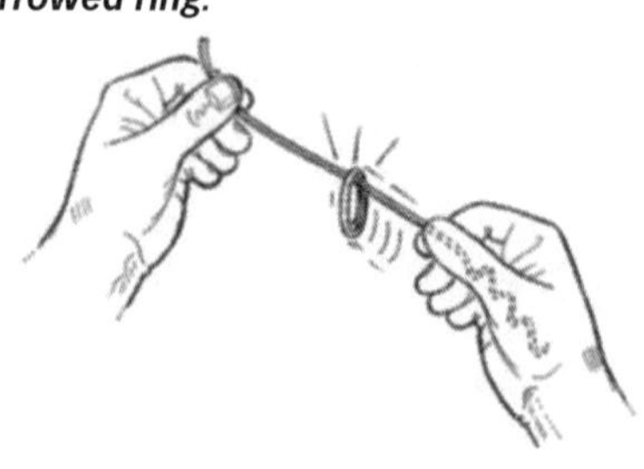

Even a broken rubber band can be used to create magic! Borrow a ring from an audience member and put it on your broken rubber band. Now grip the band in the centre with one hand, keeping the rest hidden in your hand. With your other hand, stretch out the band so that it is sloping upwards. The ring should be at the bottom of the slope, nearer to the hand with the hidden portion of rubber band. Now slowly let the band slip between your fingers, releasing the portion you concealed. The ring will creep uphill in a very magical way! The slower you let the band come out from your hand, the slower and more magical the creeping action will be.

104. UNPOPPABLE BALLOON!

Props needed: A balloon, transparent tape and push pins (younger magicians should not attempt this trick).

Blow up a balloon and place several small pieces of transparent tape over different spots on the balloon. When it is time to do the trick, show the balloon and begin pushing pins into the taped spots. Because of the tape, the balloon will not pop! Remove all the pins then finally pop the balloon by pushing a pin into an untaped spot!

105. THE VANISHING PENCIL!

Props needed: A pencil and a handkerchief.

Hold a pencil or pen in your left hand. Have an audience member drape a handkerchief over the pencil but as soon as they do, extend your left index finger and at the same time let the pencil slide down your sleeve. Count to three and have your assistant whisk the handkerchief away. On three, put your index finger back down and it will appear that the pencil has vanished!

106.THE ROLLING STONE

Props needed: A long piece of black thread, a ring and small stone or marble.

Take a long piece of black thread and tie it to a small ring. Place the ring in the centre of the table so the thread is hanging off the end of the table where you will be sitting. Now cover everything with a tablecloth. Say you can mentally control a stone and cause it to move across the table. Place a small stone (the rounder the better) on top of the ring under the tablecloth. Now pretend to concentrate as you secretly pull the thread under the table. It will look like the stone is moving on its own!

107. THE BALANCING EGG

Props needed: An egg and the same thread/ring set-up described above.

Balance the egg on end by setting it on the ring (still hidden beneath the tablecloth). When you lift the egg away, pull the thread with your other hand so that the ring will be withdrawn.

108. THE APPEARING BALL

Props needed: a short piece of flesh-coloured thread (or fishing line), a small ball and a finger ring.

The magician shows his hand absolutely empty. He reaches in the air, and "catches" a ball with his finger tips. Take a piece of thread about three inches long and tie it to the ring. Glue or tape the other end to a small rubber or plastic ball. When the ring is worn on your ring finger and your hand is held with the fingers pointing upwards, the ball hangs out of sight behind your hand. When you swing your hand upwards and turn it slightly forward, the ball will appear instantly at your finger tips!

109. THE FLYING BALL

Props needed: a ping-pong ball and a long piece of black thread (or fishing line) tied into a long loop.

A ball is held in one hand and it suddenly glides through the air to the other hand. The secret is a long loop of dark thread which is on your table with your ping-pong ball resting on it. As you pick up the ball, put your thumbs through each end of the loop. Lift your hands with the thread stretched between them and the ball appears to be floating in the air. With practice you can make the ball "float" from hand to hand!

110. THE BALANCING GOLF BALLS

Props needed: Two golf balls and a small piece of soft wax.

Balancing one golf ball on another sounds impossible and it would be if there were not a trick to it! A little piece of wax, secretly attached to the upper ball, is all that is necessary. The upper ball is pressed onto the lower ball so that the wax sticks the two balls together and the upper ball will remain, apparently balanced! Of course, you can secretly pick the wax off of the upper ball afterwards so your friends can also try this impossible feat!

111. THE ANTI-GRAVITY CUPS

Props needed: Two paper cups, a staple, a book, a newspaper and your magic wand.

Take a staple and tape it, points up, to a book (be careful not to poke yourself!). Cover the book with a small piece of newspaper so the staple can't be seen. When it's time to do the trick, take two paper cups and press them down over the ends of the staple so the points break through the newspaper. You want to be sure you have a separate cup over each end of the staple! Then take your magic wand and put it between the cups. Lift all of this up and turn the book over, while keeping the wand between the cups. The pressure of the wand against the cups and the ends of the staple will keep the cups suspended in mid-air!

112. ANOTHER ANTI-GRAVITY CUP

Props needed: A paper cup and a loop of transparent tape (or a piece of double-sided tape).

Begin by making a loop of tape (sticky side out!) and placing the loop around your thumb as though it were a ring. During your show, pick the cup up with your hand and gently but firmly press your thumb against the cup. Now, let go of the cup with your hand and it will appear to float in mid-air since the back of the cup is stuck to your thumb! You can also use a small piece of double-sided tape and simply stick it directly to the ball of your thumb!

113. AND ONE LAST ANTI-GRAVITY CUP

Props needed: A styrofoam coffee cup.

During your show, show an empty styrofoam coffee cup. Tell your audience you are going to make it float! Pick the cup up with your hand and gently press your thumb through the styrofoam and into the cup a short way (don't do this too fast — you don't want them to hear the cup breaking. Also, don't push your thumb in too far: just the tip of it will do) then let go of the cup: it will remain suspended in mid-air! Close your hand around the cup again and pull your thumb out of the hole, then cover the hole with your thumb to hide it!

114. THE ANTI-GRAVITY BOTTLE

Props needed: A small, plastic cola bottle, at least halfway full of cola.

This one is sneaky because the bottle can be fully examined at the end! Borrow a bottle of cola from a spectator. Announce you are going to make the bottle float in mid-air! Loosen the cap a bit to allow some air to escape. Then, grip the bottle in your hand. Press your thumb into the bottle just underneath the label and when an indentation form, slip your thumb up underneath the label. Now, let go of the bottle and it will remain suspended from behind by your thumb! From the front, it will appear the bottle is floating! Next, close your hand around the bottle, pull your thumb out from under the label and while you're tightening the cap again, give the bottle a little squeeze to pop the indentation that your thumb made back out. Hand the bottle back and they'll never know how you did it!

115. THE ROVING RATTLE!

Props needed: One full matchbox, three empty matchboxes and a rubber band.

Using a rubber band, attach a full box of matches to your arm and pull your sleeve down over the box. During your show, bring out three empty matchboxes. If you shake the first two boxes with your left hand, they will sound empty but if you shake the third box with your right hand it will sound full of matches! Now scramble the matchboxes and ask your audience to guess where the matches are. Whatever box they choose, shake it with your left hand to show it is "empty." Pick up one of the other boxes with your right hand and shake it saying, "Nope! The matches are here!" You can do this over and over!

116. CUT AND RESTORED NEWSPAPER

Props needed: Newspaper, scissors and rubber cement.

Begin by cutting out a thin strip of newspaper: it should only be about an inch wide but about seven inches long. Next, apply a thin layer of rubber cement to one side of the strip and allow it to dry. During your show, bring out the newspaper strip and fold it in half so the side with the rubber cement is facing the inside. Now, cut the folded part of the newspaper off of the top with a pair of scissors (or safety scissors if you are too young to use regular scissors). Now, carefully unfold the newspaper: the rubber cement will stick to itself at the point of the cut and it will appear that the newspaper strip has been restored!

117. EGG TO CONFETTI

Props needed: A hollow egg (instructions below), confetti or small pieces of cut-up paper.

Begin by having an adult help you crack a hole into one side of an egg (not the top or the bottom) and drain all of the egg out of it. You will now have a shell with a hole in one side (please do not waste the egg — use it for breakfast!). Let the shell dry out completely. Once dry, fill the egg up with confetti (you can buy confetti at a party supply store or cut some up yourself from different-coloured pieces of paper). Finally, glue a piece of paper over the hole in the egg. During your show, bring the egg out and show it to your audience, making sure the side with the hole is facing you. To your audience it will look like an ordinary egg! Now, quickly squeeze the egg in your hand and immediately throw it up in the air- confetti will rain down! The pieces of shell will blend in with the confetti so it will appear the egg has vanished! *NOTE: Never do this trick over a carpet. Only do it over a flat surface that will be easy to sweep. Always ask permission if doing this trick at someone else's house. Never throw the confetti at your audience — always throw it straight up in the air!

118. THE SPINNING EGG

Props needed: Three uncooked and one hard-boiled egg.

Two or three eggs are laid on the table and people are asked to spin them. They will find that the task is next to impossible: the eggs start to spin but topple and fall on their sides. When the magician spins an egg, it whirls like a top. One the eggs is hard-boiled. It is kept out of sight until different people are busy spinning eggs, then the magician picks up one of the eggs and takes an opportunity to replace it with the hard-boiled egg. The hard-boiled egg may be spun with ease!

119. IT'S A KNOCKOUT

Props needed: Ten red checkers and one black checker.

Ten checkers are stacked up and all are red except the fourth from the bottom, which is black.The magician stands another checker on end and by pressing down with his finger, snaps it so that it shoots against the stack of checkers. Instead of the stack falling over, the one black checker flies from the stack, while the other checkers do not fall! Because the black checker is just high enough to receive the blow from the edge of the red checker, it is knocked from the stack without upsetting the other checkers!

120. THE MOVING CHECKER

Props needed: Seven checkers, black paper, scissors, tape and a piece of paper.

A stack of about seven checkers is set up with a black checker in the middle of the red ones. The stack is covered with a paper tube and when the tube is lifted, the black checker has moved to the bottom of the stack! Before your show, cut a thin piece of black paper that will fit loosely around a checker then tape it into a loop. ALL of the checkers in the stack are red ones, but the centre one has the ring around it and appears to be black. The stack should be slightly uneven. The paper tube is used to straighten the stack and when the stack is straightened, the black ring will naturally drop to the bottom checker.

121. THE MOVING STACKS

Props needed: Black and red checkers, black and red paint and two pieces of paper.

Two slacks of checkers are used in this trick—one stack is red and the other is black. Each stack is wrapped in a cylinder of paper with the top twisted over to hide the checkers from above. The red stack is placed several feet away from the black stack and the magician commands them to change places. When he lifts the paper cylinders, the checkers have obeyed the order, the black being where the red were supposed to be, and vice versa! Two special checkers are required for this trick: one is red with the bottom painted black and the other is black with the bottom painted red. The prepared checkers are the bottom ones of the stacks. After each stack is covered with a paper cylinder, the magician closes the tops of the cylinders and tilts the cylinders to allow the audience a glimpse of the bottom of the lowermost checker.Thus, the black stack is identified as red and the red stack is identified as black.

122. THE MAGNETIC DICE

Props needed: Two dice.

A pair of dice are placed on the table, and one die is placed on top of the other. When the upper die is lifted, the lower one clings to it as though magnetized. Place the first die on the table with the "one" side facing upward. Next, lick the tip of your finger and apply it to the "one" side of the upper die. When both of the "one" sides of the dice are pressed together, they will stick and they can be lifted together as thought they are magnetized.

123. THE DOMI-KNOWS

Props needed: A set of dominoes.

Place a set of dominoes on the table and invite two or three people to line up the dominoes, as though playing a game. Before they begin, you write something on a piece of paper and lay it on the table in full view. When the game is over, there will be two ends to the row of dominoes. Let's suppose the number on one end is five and on the other end it's three. When the piece of paper is unfolded, it will show the numbers five and three! You have foretold what the end numbers will be! Before your show, secretly remove one of the dominoes (not a double). The numbers on the domino (in this case 3 and 5) will tell you what the end numbers will be!

MENTAL MAGIC

124. I CAN READ YOUR MIND

Props needed: A secret accomplice!

The next couple of effects will require a secret accomplice. Make sure that it is somebody you trust will never reveal the secret of your magic effects! For the first demonstration of mind-reading, pick a person at random to be your helper. You are actually going to pick your accomplice! Tell the audience that you are going to leave the room and that this helper must select one object in the room and when you come back you will try and guess which one it is. When you come back in, you will ask your helper to point to different objects to help you focus your powers. Your helper has been told in advance to make the fourth object the chosen one. Don't stop them as soon as you know the object, let them carry on pointing at a few more before you say, "I've got it!" and announce the correct object.

125. THE BAFFLING REPEAT

Props needed: A secret accomplice!

If you repeat the above trick too many times, people could start to catch on. So, to keep the smart ones from getting it, you and your secret helper should do some planning in advance.The first time you do the trick, your helper could point to the fourth object. The next time they could point to the third and then finally the sixth. Doing the effect four times is enough for any audience. Your secret numbering code will have them totally puzzled as to how you are always able to guess the correct object!

126. BACK IN BLACK

Props needed: A secret accomplice!

Another way to do I Can Read Your Mind is to have your secret assistant point to something black right before he points to the chosen object. Whenever you see your assistant point to something in the room that's black, you will know the next object is the chosen object!

127. SILENT TRANSMISSION: ONE TO TWENTY

Props needed: A secret accomplice!

You will need a secret accomplice for this trick. Start by announcing that you are going to leave the room, and while you are away everybody is to choose a number. When they have all agreed upon a number, they are to concentrate on it and call you back in. Ask them to make the number between one and twenty so it is not too big. When you enter the room, point to your secret assistant and say, "You look as though you may be good at transmitting thoughts, so I'll use you for the effect!" Put your hands on either side of your assistant's head as you say, "I will now link our two minds together!" As you pretend to concentrate, your secret helper tightens and loosens his jaw the same number of times as the chosen number! Your hands will cover any signs of the motion, and you'll be able to amaze everyone by correctly guessing the secretly chosen number!

128. SILENT TRANSMISSION: ONE TO A HUNDRED

Props needed: A secret accomplice!

With a small addition to the previous trick, you can give the audience their choice of any number from one to a hundred. Since you don't want to be counting eighty-five jaw motions, you will have to cheat a little. First, your secret helper tightens and loosens their jaw for the first figure of the number. If the number were eighty-five, they would tighten their jaw eight times,then they should pause for a moment, then tighten and loosen five times. Using this technique, you can even fool people who know the original one to twenty version, as they won't be able to understand how you were able to jump to the large numbers so quickly!

129. PREDICTED COLOURS

Props needed: Paper and a pen or pencil.

Before your show, take four pieces of paper and write the name of a different colour on each one: yellow, blue, green and red. Fold up the pieces of paper and put them in your pocket in that order. During your show, bring out a pad of paper and pencil and tell the audience you are going to write a list of colours. Then say out loud green, blue, red and yellow as you write them down. Then ask a helper to think of any one of the colours. When they tell you their colour, you can instantly produce the correct slip of paper to prove that you knew in advance just the one they would think of!

130. THE MIND-READING ENVELOPE

Props needed: Two envelopes, paper or card stock and a pen or pencil.

Here's another way to do the above effect. For this trick you will need to make a special envelope. Before your show, get two envelopes and carefully and neatly glue them face to face, so that they are perfectly aligned and the two flaps are facing out on both of them. Then take a thick piece of heavy paper or card stock and in pencil on one side of it write "You will choose red." On the other side write "You will choose yellow." Put this in one of the envelopes.On the other piece of paper write "You will choose green" and on the other side write "You will choose blue," and then place it in the other envelope. Put this special envelope in your pocket. During the show, ask a helper, just as you did before to name one of the four colours, when they do, all you need to do is take out the envelope and open the correct side and take the card out from the correct side, not letting them see that there are two envelopes glued together or that there is a colour on each side of the card.

131. THE APPEARING CARD IN ENVELOPE

Props needed: Two envelopes and a playing card.

Once again make a special envelope as you did for the previous trick. This time prior to your show place the Ace Of Spades from a deck of cards into it and place the envelope into your pocket. When you are ready to perform, tell your audience that you are going to magically and invisibly place an Ace inside of the envelope. Now, show them the empty envelope. Then pretend to put an invisible ace in it. As you put the envelope down on the table you will have to turn it over, without anyone seeing you do it! Then make a magic pass over the envelope and say, "I think something is in the envelope now." Then open the envelope and take out the playing card!

132. WHAT'S ON THE PAPER?

Props needed: A piece of paper and a pen or pencil.

The magician tells a person to write anything he chooses on a piece of paper then to fold the paper and put it on the floor. To prevent the magician from seeing anything, the person is told to put his foot on the folded paper. The magician announces that although he cannot see the writing, he can tell exactly what is on the paper. Closing his eyes and summoning up all of his mental ability he suddenly announces, "your foot." The spectator can't argue with that!

133. THE PSYCHIC CELL PHONE

Props needed: A phone and a friend with a phone.

Before your show have a friend who has access to a cell phone help you out with the Three Dice Prediction. Tell your friend that he or she will be getting a phone call asking forThe Great Rambini and they are to say to the person they will be speaking on the phone with "the total of the dice is 21!" Instead of revealing the number 21, have them call The Great Rambini for an amazing revelation! This is an incredible effect that can be done anytime, because once you have let your friend in on the trick then anytime someone calls them asking for The Great Rambini they will know what to do!

134. I PREDICT

Props needed: A deck with a force card on top, a coffee mug and three small pieces of paper.

For this great mentalism effect you will need a deck with a force card on top, a coffee mug and three small pieces of paper. Begin by telling your spectators that you will predict three things chosen at random. To start, have a spectator cut the deck. You will perform the Cross-Cut Force at this point but leave the deck criss-crossed on the table- do not reveal the chosen card yet! Now, say you are going to write your first predicTion down: an object in the room. What you are really doing is writing down your force card! Fold this paper up and drop it into the coffee mug. Now ask the spectators to name something in the room. Let's say they choose, "chair." Pick up another piece of paper and say that you are going to write down a random number. Of course, you write, "chair" on the paper, fold it up and place it in the mug. Finally, say you are going to write the name of the card the spectators have chosen earlier: since the card hasn't been revealed yet, no one knows what it is! On the last slip of paper, write down the number that the audience has just given you, fold it up and place it in the mug. Now, pick up the top of the deck and show the force card to your audience. Now dump all of the papers out of the mug. Unfold them and your audience will be astonished to see that all three papers correctly predicted the chosen objects!

135. A MAGICAL MESSAGE

Props needed: A paper bag, a pen and around ten pieces of paper.

On a piece of paper write, "The chosen object will be a chair!" and put it in your pocket. Also for this effect you will need a paper bag, a pen and around ten pieces of paper. 1. Ask your helpers to call out things they could see in a house and you pretend to write these objects down on the pieces of paper. Actually you simply write "chair" on every one of them but don't let your helpers see you doing this! Crumple up each piece of paper after you have written on it and drop it into the bag. Shake up all the pieces in the bag and ask a helper to reach in and pick one out.They open it up and, of course read out the word chair. Now take your prediction out of your pocket. Not only has a magical message appeared but it's correctly predicted the chosen object!

136. YOUR NUMBER'S UP

Props needed: A pad and pen or pencil.

On a piece of paper write, "The number will be 1089!" and seal this into an envelope (if you'd like, you can write, "Magic Prediction" on it). During your show bring out a pad and a pen. Say to one of your helpers, "I want you to think of a three digit number but all the numbers must be different and the first number must be higher than the last one!" Write their number down at the top of your pad. Underneath it write his number backwards (so if his number is 754 you would write 457 for example). Now subtract the smaller number from the larger one. If you aren't so good at math you might want to use a calculator here! Using our example numbers from above the answer would be 297. Write this number down. Now under our new number write this one backwards to give us 792. Finally, add the last two numbers (297 and 792) and you'll get 1089. Whatever three digit number they start with, provided they follow your simple rules, the answer will always be 1089 meaning that your mathemagical prediction is always right!

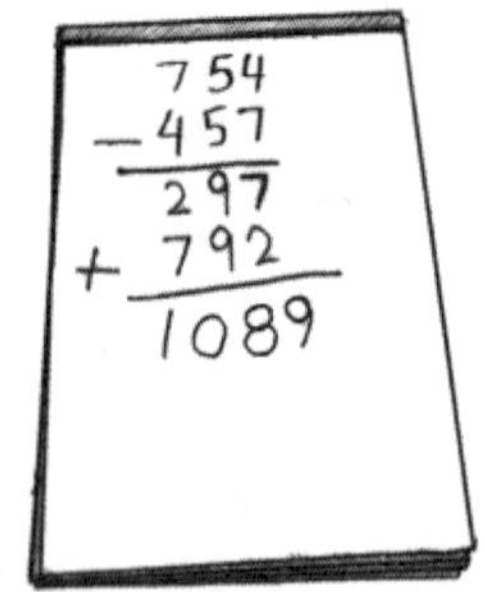

137. THE 1089 BOOK TEST

Props needed: A pad, pen or pencil and a book with more than 108 pages.

Choose a book from your book shelf and turn to page 108. Count through the words at the top of page 108 until you get to the ninth word and write it on a piece of paper. Now, seal this piece of paper in an envelope. During your show, do the trick Your Number's Up the same way except this time, you're not going to reveal "1089" as the prediction. Instead, bring out the same book you used at the beginning of this trick and tell the person to turn to page 108 in the book and read the ninth word from the top.When they do, bring out your sealed envelope and have them open it, revealing that you knew what their chosen word would be all along!

138. THE PSYCHIC CRAYONS

Props needed: A box of crayons or coloured pencils or coloured markers.

Show an ordinary box of crayons (coloured pencils and markers also work) and tell your audience you can guess any colour that is handed to you behind your back. Put both of your hands behind your back and have an audience member hand you any colour. Quickly colour a little bit of the crayon onto your thumbnail then bring that hand around and quickly glance at your thumbnail to see the colour of the crayon!

139. MAGIC CLOCK

Props needed: A non-digital clock or watch and a pencil (or your magic wand).

You can discover a number that has just been thought of by a helper. To do this, you will need a clock or watch. Ask your helper to think of any number from one to twelve. Tell the spectator you are now going to tap a pencil against the numbers on the clock. As you do this, they are to start with the number they are thinking of and add one to it each time you make a tap. So if they were thinking of the number nine, they would count ten, eleven, twelve and so on each tap of your pencil. When they reach twenty they should call out 'Stop!' For the first seven taps, you may tap on any numbers of the clock face. On your eighth tap, you must tap your wand on the number twelve of the clock face. Then continue tapping numbers in backwards order around the dial (eleven, ten, nine, eight and so on). When they call out stop, you may both be astonished to find that the pencil is right on their number!

140. THE HYPNOTIZED ARM

Props needed: A helper from the audience!

Ask your helper to stand with side against a wall or door and say that you are going to hypnotize their arm! Ask them to push as hard as they can with their arm against the wall for about forty-five seconds. As you do this you can say, "I just want to make sure that you don't have the strength to be able to push over a wall. Arms that strong are tough to hypnotize!" When the time is up tell them that their arm has been hypnotized into rising upwards and ask them to stand away from the wall. They just won't be able to stop their arm creepily rising upwards!

141. THE HYPNOTIZED LEG

Props needed: A helper from the audience!

Tell your audience that you will need a volunteer. Tell them that you will put a hypnotic spell over someone and be in full control of their leg! Now tell them that using only the power of your mind, you will cause their leg to do whatever their hand is doing! First, have them lift their left leg and make clockwise circles with it. Instruct them to now make counter-clockwise circles with their left arm. Point out that their leg is now making counter-clockwise circles! Now, tell them to start making clockwise circles with their leg again, while holding their left arm still. Once their leg is going, tell them to draw a stick-figure in the air with their left hand- again, their leg will begin to draw the stick-figure too! This trick is actually science: it is very hard for a person to control their leg movements while doing something with their arms so their brain will automatically copy their arm motions to their legs!

142. SECRETS REVEALED

Props needed: A regular sheet of printer paper torn in four pieces and four pens or pencils.

Before your show, get a regular-sized, 8-1/2 X 11" piece of paper and fold it into quarters. Then, tear the paper into four pieces, along the fold lines. You will now have four pieces of paper that have two regular edges and two torn edges. Save the other three pieces because you will only need one for this trick. During your show, choose four spectators and tell them that you are going to guess their secrets! Bring out your specially prepared paper. You are now going to tear it into four pieces and give all four pieces to your spectators to write a secret on. Have them give you back all four pieces face-down. Shuffle them up behind your back too, if you'd like. Now, read each secret and immediately tell who's it was! How? Each piece of paper will be unique: the piece on the bottom left will have two straight edges and two torn edges. The piece on the bottom right will have 3 torn sides and one short straight side. The piece on the top left will have 3 torn sides and one long straight side. The piece on the top right will have four torn sides. Just remember who you give each piece to and you will immediately know who wrote which secret!

143. YET MORE MIND READING

Props needed: Ten playing cards, a pencil or your magic wand and a secret helper.

Ten playing cards are laid out on your table and, while you are out of the room, one of the cards is thought of by your helpers. You return and get one member of your audience to tap the cards one at a time with a pencil. You can immediately tell them the chosen card every time! How? The ten playing cards are laid out in the same way that the pips (the design on the face of the card) are on a ten spot card (two columns of four with a mini column of two between them). One of the cards, it doesn't matter which has to be a ten spot card. The other secret is that the helper who taps the cards is your over-worked secret pal! Although it looks as though they tap the cards the same every time

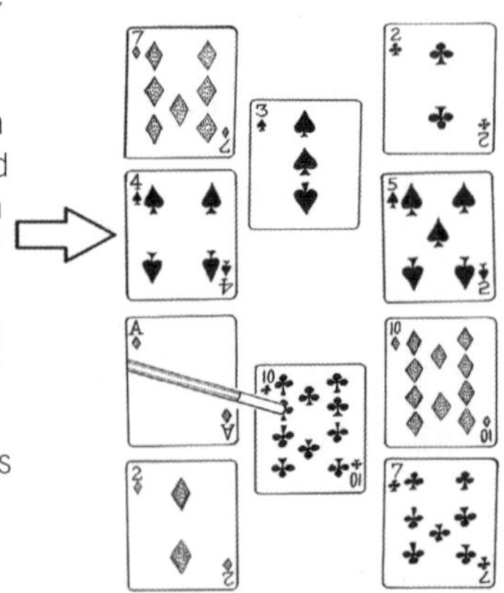

there is one very subtle difference. When they tap the ten spot they tap the pip on the card that is in the same position as the chosen card! As soon as they tap that ten spot you know the chosen card! Don't shout out the card; let them finish tapping all ten cards before getting it right. You can repeat this over and over and, because the method is so sly, it gets more and more baffling!

RESTAURANT MAGIC

144. SUSPENDED SALT

Props needed: A salt shaker and a toothpick.

Now we'll use an ordinary toothpick as a hidden magic gimmick! Put a salt or peppershaker out on your table. Now have a toothpick hidden behind your first finger (held in place by your thumb) as you touch the top of the saltshaker. Secretly push the toothpick into one of the holes on top of the shaker making sure that it goes firmly in. If you now lift your finger the shaker will magically appear to be sticking to your finger! Using your other hand pull the shaker away from the toothpick and put it onto your table. Casually ditch the toothpick in your pocket.

145. UNBROKEN

Props needed: Two toothpicks and a cloth napkin or handkerchief.

For this illusion, you will need a handkerchief or cloth napkin and two toothpicks. Before your show, push one of the toothpicks into the left hand corner hem of the handkerchief. No one is to know about this secret hidden toothpick! During you show, unfold the handkerchief onto a table and display the other toothpick as you place it in the centre of the handkerchief. Fold the handkerchief around the loose toothpick, so that the hidden toothpick is about centre of the handkerchief. Take hold of the hidden toothpick through the material and place that part of the handkerchief into your helper's hand. Note: Make sure that you have folded the handkerchief in such a way so the other toothpick won't fall out! Request that a helper break the toothpick through the cloth. Ask them, "Did you feel it break, did you hear it break?" When they confirm that they did, open the handkerchief onto the table to show the unbroken toothpick inside!

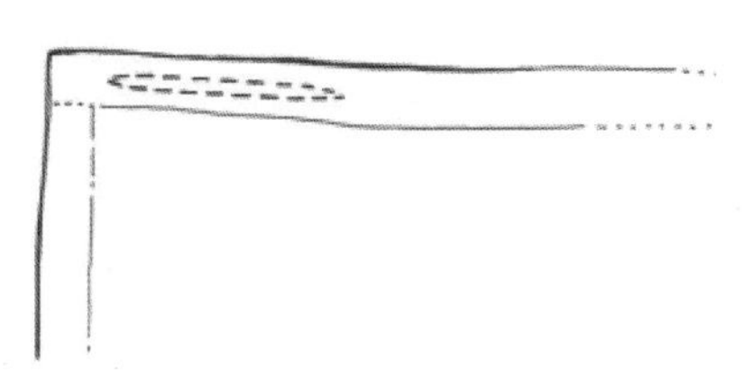

146. BROKEN AND RESTORED TOOTHPICK

Props needed: Two toothpicks.

Start off by secretly preparing your gimmick. This is done by simply breaking a toothpick in half. During your show, hand out a whole toothpick for examination. After the toothpick is given back, hold it with the fingertips of your left hand. Bring your right hand (with the half piece hidden in between your fingers) towards your left hand. Covering the toothpick in your left hand for a brief moment, slide part of the toothpick in your left hand further behind your fingers so that about half of it can still be seen. Act as if you're breaking the toothpick. To display the broken toothpick, show the half protruding toothpick in your left hand and the half toothpick in your right hand. To restore the toothpick, mention how you need to build up static in the pieces. Display the half piece in your right hand then rub it on your left elbow as if you're building up static. Next, display the half-protruding toothpick in your left hand; rub it on your right elbow (right hand raised towards the right side of your neck). As you rub the left-hand piece to your elbow, ditch the half piece down your shirt collar. Now, bring both hands together, as if you're connecting the pieces then slide out the toothpick in your left hand so that the whole toothpick can now be seen. The toothpick is now fully examinable again.

147. POCKET PICK

Props needed: Two toothpicks.

If you want to prepare for this trick well in advance and want to have your hands available for other tricks prior to performing the Broken and Restored Toothpick, start the trick out with the half piece in your pocket. Openly hand out the whole toothpick for examination. While the audience is examining the toothpick, casually reach into your pocket to retrieve the half piece. Afterwards, just place the half piece into the same holding position as in the first version and continue as before.

148. VANISHING AND APPEARING TOOTHPICK

Props needed: A toothpick and a piece of transparent tape.

Attach the toothpick to your thumbnail with a small piece of tape so that the point is facing downward toward the knuckle. To make the toothpick appear, curl your fingers forward (almost into a fist) then bend your thumb forward so that your thumbnail and toothpick rest in the crotch of your pointer finger. To make the toothpick vanish, simply extend your thumb (pointing it upward) and extend all your other fingers of the same hand to show your hand empty. Be sure to keep the padding of your thumb (the finger print portion) facing your audience as to keep the toothpick out of sight.

149. WATCH WHERE YOU'RE THROWING

Props needed: A toothpick and a piece of transparent tape.

When the toothpick is made to vanish, be sure to not look at your thumb. That would give away the method. Instead, imagine as if you're actually flinging the toothpick upwards, for example. If you were to do that, your eyes would follow the toothpick as it flew. So practice "following" the toothpick with your eyes to where it should be if you actually tossed it, up to the point where it disappears.

150. THE SAD TOOTHPICK

Props needed: A toothpick and a piece of wet tissue or paper napkin.

For this trick, you will pretend to get annoyed with a toothpick and it will appear to cry. Before your show, prepare by hiding a piece of wet tissue paper between your thumb and first two fingers. Don't let anybody see it, of course! Now grab hold of a toothpick between your fingers and thumb, making sure

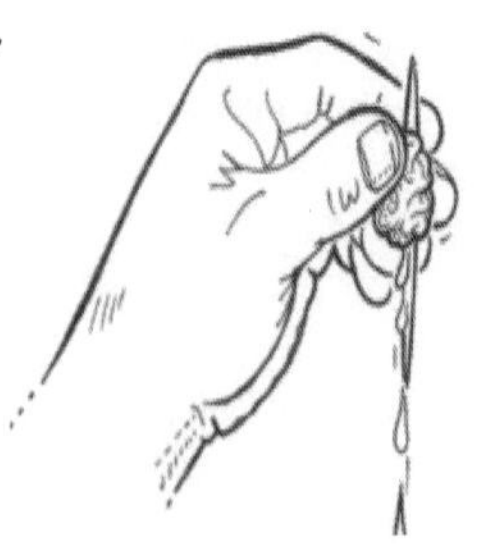

that it is resting on the hidden tissue. During your show, pretend to get annoyed at the toothpick, squeeze it against the tissue paper, forcing drops of water to run off of it. Say, "Aw! The poor little thing is crying!" Put the toothpick on the table and casually ditch the tissue into your pocket as you finish.

151. THE MAGNETIC TOOTHPICK

Props needed: Two flat toothpicks.

Place a flat (not rounded) toothpick on a table and balance another toothpick across the centre so neither end of the top toothpick is touching the table. Tell your audience that the toothpick is magnetic and is only attracted to your finger. Hold your finger slightly off to the right of the toothpick. Then secretly and quietly blow the left side of the toothpick so it moves toward your finger. It will appear that the toothpick is drawn to your finger!

152. THE SNEAKY COUNT

Props needed: Ten toothpicks and a pencil.

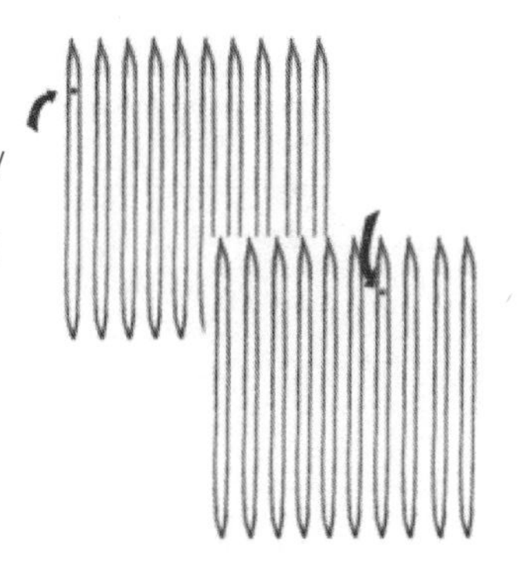

Get ten toothpicks and on one of them make a tiny secret mark on both sides so that you can tell this one apart from the others. Make the mark as small as possible with a pencil so that you are the only one who knows that it is there. During your show, bring out the ten toothpicks and put them out in a line side by side. Make sure that your secretly marked toothpick is the first one on the left hand end of the row. That means the secret marked toothpick is on your left, but your audience's right. Say that you will turn your back and that one of them is to move a number of toothpicks between one and ten, one at a time, from the right to the left end of the row. This means the first toothpick they will move is the secret toothpick. When they have finished you turn back and say, " I'm going to tell you just how many toothpicks you moved!" As you say this, look for your secretly marked toothpick and counting it as 'one' count how many there are to the right end (your right) of the row and then tell them that's how many were moved!

153. HOPPING TOOTHPICKS

Props needed: Two toothpicks.

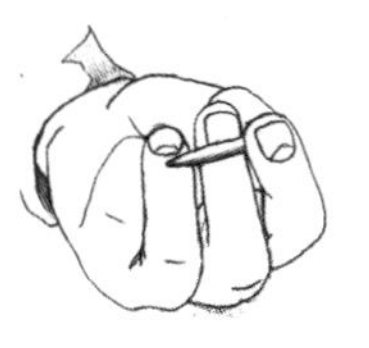

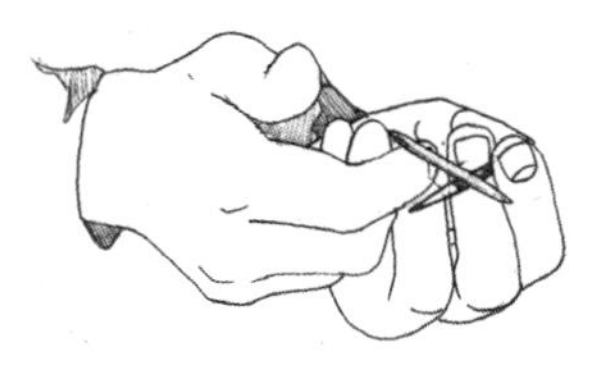

This is a very eerie effect that will drive your friends wild as they try to figure out just what is going on! Hold one tooth pick exactly as shown. It is very important to get the grip just right or the effect will not work. Notice especially how the toothpick is resting against the nail of your second finger. Now balance a second toothpick on top resting it between the first finger of the other hand and the end of the held toothpick. Say, "My magical pulse is so strong that sometimes it can become visible!" Now slowly rub the held toothpick up against the second fingernail. Do this very slowly and the top toothpick will hop up and down in a very strange way.

154. BANANA SHENANIGANS

Props needed: A banana and a toothpick.

Before your show, push the toothpick through the peel of a banana and work it back and forth through the banana so it cuts a slice in the banana. Do this all down the side of the banana, cutting it into several slices. During your show, bring out the banana and say you love bananas but you prefer to eat them sliced. Make a magical "cutting" gesture over the banana and shock your audience by peeling it and having the banana fall out in slices!

155. VANISHING SUGAR

Props needed: A sugar packet.

Prior to performing this trick, cut a small slit into a sugar packet (through only one layer of the paper wrapper) towards the top of the wrapper and empty all of the sugar out of the packet. Once the packet is emptied out, turn it so the slit is towards the top of the packet. Now place the packet on the table or in a sugar packet container (being sure to keep track of which packet is the empty one), so that the slit is away from the audience. When you're ready to perform, pick up your gimmicked sugar packet and tear it open along the slit that you originally made. Make a fist with your left hand and pretend to pour the "sugar" into your fist, being sure to not leave any space between the sugar packet and your fist or your audience will see that no sugar is actually pouring out! Once all the sugar is believed to have been poured into your hand, completely close up your fist. Wave your hand (or a magic wand) over your closed fist. After a magical moment, open your hand to show that the sugar has completely vanished!

156. THE CONVINCER

Props needed: A sugar packet.

As an added convincer, try to keep a very small portion of the sugar in the sugar packet. This will make it so that when you perform this trick and are pouring the sugar into your fist, there will actually be a bit of sugar on the opening of your fist and anywhere else that sugar would actually fall... This will convince the audience that there actually was sugar in the packet!

157. SUGAR SHENANIGANS

Props needed: Two sugar packets.

Why not have audience members try this trick with you? Pick up your secretly empty sugar packet and have them pick up a normal sugar packet, then invite them to do as you do. Perform the trick as instructed above. You'll have magically vanished the sugar. Your audience member won't and instead, they'll be left with a sugary mess to have to clean up afterwards!

158. THE UNCUTTABLE STRING!

Props needed: A piece of string, a straw and scissors.

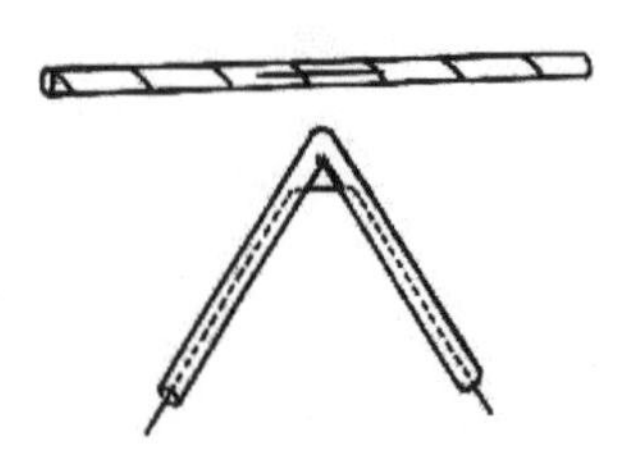

For this trick you will need a straw and a piece of string longer than the straw. Start by having an adult cut a slit in the centre of the straw. During your show, bring out the straw and the string and say that the string is uncuttable! To prove this, drop one end of the string into the straw and thread it through. Once it's all the way through, bend the straw in half in the centre. Make sure the slit is facing DOWN. Now, pull on the ends of the string- this forces the string into the slit and away from the centre of the straw. Have a spectator cut the centre of the straw with a pair of safety scissors. Now, slide the two halves off of the string and show that the string is still intact! It's uncuttable!

159. TELEKINETIC STRAW

Props: A straw and a drinking glass.

Take a regular drinking straw, remove the wrapper and balance it on the bottom of a drinking glass. Now, hold your hands at the ends of the straw but slightly away from them so you are not touching the straw. Slowly move your hands and the straw will move with them. Telekinetic energy? Not quite! As you remove the straw from the wrapper, pinch the straw as you pull the wrapper down and off. This will build up a charge of static electricity inside the straw which will be repelled by the static electricity in your body!

160. THE GLASS THROUGH THE TABLE!

Props needed: A coin, a glass and a paper placemat (newspaper works too).

This is a great trick to do in a restaurant! Tell your friends that you are going to make a coin penetrate through the table. Place a coin on the table and put an empty glass mouth-down over the coin. Now take your paper placemat (if you're doing this at home just use a sheet of newspaper) and cover the glass with it. Press it down all around the glass so you can see the shape of the glass. Now pat your hand on the top of the glass and lift the glass, with the placemat still around it, up and over your lap. Point out that something must have gone wrong because the coin is still there. While your friends are looking at the coin, secretly let the glass slip out of the placemat and into your lap. Because the placemat is the same shape as the glass, they will not think the glass is no longer there! Place the now-empty placemat back over the coin and smash it very hard with your hand so the placemat crumples flat against the table. Now reach into your lap and pull the glass out saying that you don't know your own strength! When you first practice this trick, use a plastic glass until you're confident enough to use a real one!

161. THE BALANCING GLASS

Props needed: Two playing cards, transparent tape, scissors and a plastic cup.

Take two cards from an ordinary deck (preferably the Jokers so you don't ruin the rest of the deck) and cut one of the cards in half. Now, using some transparent tape, tape the cut edge of the half-card to the centre of the back of the full card. If you did this correctly, your card will now form a little tripod that stands up on its own when the flap is swung out but looks like a regular card when the flap is flat. During your show, bring out your secretly gimmicked card and lay it flat on the table with the flap side down. No one is to see this flap! Next, bring out a drinking glass. Tell your friends that using magic, you will balance the glass on the edge of the card! Stand the card up on the table, secretly swinging the flap out behind the card, forming the tripod (the flap should be facing YOU, not the audience) and rest the glass on top of the card and flap. When you take your hands away, it will look like the glass is balancing on top of an ordinary playing card! Take the glass back off and quickly fold the flap flat against the card before laying the card down again.

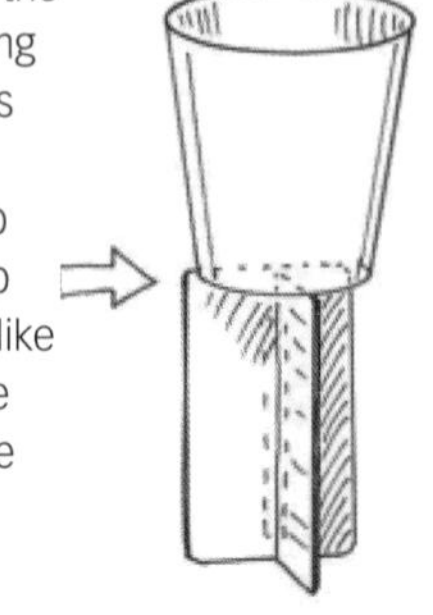

162. SALTY

Props needed: Salt, pepper and a comb.

Pour a small pile of pepper onto a table napkin then add some salt to it. Don't add too much salt, just a sprinkle is fine. Mix the salt and pepper together then ask a friend how long they think it would take them to separate the salt and pepper. Offer to teach them how to do it in less than two seconds! To do this take a plastic comb and comb it through your hair for a few seconds. Quickly hold it right above the pile and the salt will jump up and cling to the comb leaving the pepper behind!

163. COIN TO SUGAR PACKET

Props needed: A sugar packet and a borrowed coin.

Like the set-up to Vanishing Sugar, prior to performing this trick, cut a slit into the sugar packet but his time, DON'T pour out all the sugar! Take a coin that fits into the packet and insert it into the slit of the packet. Once the coin is in the packet, keep the packet held upward. Place it into a sugar packet holder in which all the other sugar packets are kept. When you're ready to perform, ask the audience for a coin (matching the one you point into the sugar packet). Have them place the coin on the table. Reach for the coin with your right hand and slide it towards you until the coin falls onto your lap. Continue by bringing your empty hand up (as if you still have the coin in your hand) then pretend to put the coin into your left hand. Wave your right hand over your left hand, then open your left hand to show that the coin has vanished. After showing both hands empty, reach for your prepared sugar packet with the coin in it and tear it open. Pour out the contents to show that the borrowed coin has appeared in the sugar packet!

164. LET THEM OPEN THE PACKET

Props Needed: A sugar packet, a coin and a glue stick.

For this version of the trick, you'll need to take split a sugar packet at its seams. This just takes some practice and some advance working at home. Begin by picking up a sugar packet and finding a corner that's easy to split. If you don't find one, you can make one by teasing a corner of the packet until you find that the packet starts to split. Gently open the packet, being sure to not spill any of the sugar, insert the coin and reseal the packet with a glue stick. Now, during your performance, you can hand the sugar packet to your spectator and they can tear the packet open themselves without it appearing that the packet has been gimmicked in any way!

165. SIGNED COIN TO SUGAR PACKET

Props Needed: A sugar packet, a coin, a marker and a glue stick.

Perform the Borrowed Coin to Sugar Packet, but with a signed coin! This would really throw your audience off from ever thinking that you could possibly be using a duplicate coin somehow! Set up the trick the same way but initial the coin with a marker before sealing it into the sugar packet. During your show, write your initials on the back of the borrowed coin with a marker before dropping it into your lap. Proceed with the trick as above and when they open the packet they will be astonished!

166. BILL IN SUGAR PACKET

Props Needed: A sugar packet, a bill and a glue stick.

You can perform another variation of this trick with a dollar bill in the sugar packet instead of a coin. Begin by teasing open a sugar packet like you did in, "Let Them Open The Packet." Next, fold up a dollar bill this way: fold the bill in half width-wise, then in half width-wise again. From there, fold it in thirds and in thirds again. This will make it tiny enough to fit inside of a sugar packet. Glue the packet shut with a glue stick and put it in with the regular sugar packets. During your performance, vanish the dollar bill (a double-backed envelope works well for this) or simply put it in your pocket. Now, have an audience member open the sugar packet to retrieve the bill!

167. CARD IN SUGAR PACKET

Props Needed: A sugar packet, a card and a glue stick.

For this trick you will need a deck of cards and one duplicate card. Let's say the duplicate card is the Five Of Hearts. Fold a 5H up and insert it into a sugar packet as you learned earlier. During your show, force the 5H and then vanish it (again, a double-backed envelope works well for this). Have a spectator open the sugar packet and reveal the chosen card!

COIN AND MONEY MAGIC

168. ODDLY EVEN

Props needed: A coin of 10 cents, 5 cents and five 1 cent coins.

The magician holds several coins in his hand and asks a spectator to guess whether the money is odd or even. The person will always make the wrong guess! The magician simply uses a 10 cent coin, a 5 cent coinl and five 1 cent coin. If the person says "even," the magician opens his hand and counts the coins, showing that he has seven—an odd number. If the person says "odd," the magician totals the amount: ten cents, five cents, and five for the pennies for a total of twenty cents, which is even!

169. YEARLY BELOVED

Props needed: Two coins with matching years.

This trick requires a bit of memory. Don't worry, all you'd have to memorize is four numbers. A year, to be exact... Which shouldn't be difficult at all! More than likely, you'd be memorizing "19" and two more numbers, or "20" and two more numbers, as coins you'll see on a daily basis are from the 1900's or 2000's. Take a coin (we'll say a quarter for this example) and memorize the year. Once you've got that out of the way, you'll be ready to perform! Start by having the coin you memorized the year to hidden in your right hand.

Ask an audience member for a coin and have them place the coin on the table. With the coin hidden in your hand, reach for the coin and slide it towards you until the coin falls onto your lap. Continue by bringing your hand up with the memorized coin. Next, close your hand around the coin and turn to the audience member and slowly reveal each number in the year on the coin. Hand the coin back to them to have them confirm the date is correct!

170. THE SAD COIN

Props needed: A coin and a piece of wet tissue or paper napkin.

Just as you pretended to make a toothpick cry, you can use the same moves to make a coin cry. Once again hide the wet tissue paper between your thumb and first two fingers. Get a large coin such as a quarter and hold it with the same fingers, making sure the tissue cannot be seen. Say that you are going to squeeze the coin so hard it will start to cry. Squeeze the coin against the tissue and after it cries put everything in your pocket!

171. UPSIDE-DOWN MONEY

Props needed: A bill.

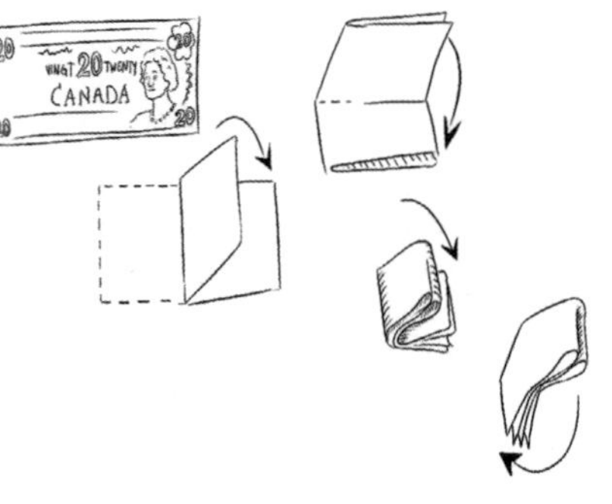

1. Take a dollar bill or, if you don't have one, see if somebody will lend you one. Promising to give it back is always a help! Hold it with Queen Elizabeth's head the right way up so your helper can see it.
2. Fold the note in half from left to right, facing you.
3. Next fold it in half from top to bottom towards you.
4. Now fold it once more from left to right.
5. Unfold the lower portion of the packet to the left then unfold the bill just as you folded it but in reverse to open it up. You may fool yourself the first time when you see that Queen Elizabeth is now upside down!

172. THE APPEARING COIN

Props needed: A coin, a glass of water and a plate or saucer.

Place a quarter on the table. Now put a glass full of water on top of the coin. Finally place a plate or saucer on top of the glass. You may astonish yourself the first time you try this because you won't be able to see the coin! Having set everything ask a friend what is in the glass. They'll say, "Water," of course. Now ask them what is under the glass. They'll say, "Nothing!" Snap your fingers and lift up the glass and saucer to show your amazing appearing coin!

173. THE FRICTION COIN SPIN

Props needed: A large coin and your fingers!

Tell your audience you can spin a coin with friction! Start by holding a large coin (a quarter or larger) on its edge against the table with your right index finger. Now rub your left index finger back and forth across your right index finger. Using your left thumb, quickly strike the side of the coin as you rub your left index finger toward your right index fingernail. At the same time, lift your right index finger and the coin will spin off across the table as though the "friction" from rubbing your finger caused the coin to spin!

174. CAPPED COIN

Props needed: Three bottle caps, a coin that will fit under the caps, a short piece of fishing line and glue or tape.

Before your show, take a short piece of fishing line and tape or glue it to the underside of a small coin or button so the fishing line sticks out about a half-inch from the edge of the coin. Since fishing line is almost invisible, you are the only one who will notice it! During your show, bring out the coin or button and three bottle caps. Place the coin/ button on the table and turn around. Ask someone from the audience to place one of the bottle caps over the coin/button and place the other two on the table as well. Tell the audience member to scramble the caps around as much as they like! When you turn around, simply look for the short piece of fishing line sticking out from underneath the cap and you will always know which bottle cap is hiding the coin!

175. CHOPPED TO BITS

Props needed: Three envelopes, a pair of scissors and two bill sized pieces of paper.

For this trick you will need three envelopes, a pair of scissors and two bill sized pieces of paper. On the back of one envelope, you are going to make a small, secret mark with a pen or pencil. Put it somewhere inconspicuous so no one else will see it but you can immediately detect it! During your show, bring out the three envelopes and the two pieces of paper. Ask to borrow a bill — if you can borrow a large bill like a twenty or fifty the trick will be even funnier! Fold the two pieces of paper and the bill into quarters. Place the bill into the marked envelope and seal it, then place the pieces of paper into their own separate envelopes and seal them too. Turn around and ask a spectator to shuffle the envelopes. Once the envelopes are shuffled, turn back around and pick one envelope up. If there is no mark on it, take out the scissors and cut it into small pieces (if you are too young to handle scissors, use safety scissors or have an adult cut the envelope up for you). If the envelope DOES have the mark, place it to the side and continue on. Pick up the second envelope — if there is no mark, cut it up. If this turns out to be the marked envelope, place it to the side. Finally, pick up the third envelope and proceed as above: unmarked = cut, marked = place to the side. At the end, you will have one solid envelope and two cut-up envelopes. Hand the solid envelope to the spectator to open and retreive his bill!

176. SUPER BALANCING COIN

Props needed: A large coin and a new dollar bill.

Begin with a new dollar bill — it needs to be as new and crisp as you can possibly get. First, fold the bill in half from top to bottom. Next, fold the bill in half from side to side. Place the bill on the table so that the folded edge is facing up and the bill is in a "V" formation. Now, balance a large coin in the middle of the "V." The next part might even amaze you- slowly pull both ends of the bill apart, straight-

ening out the bill. The coin will continue to balance on the centre of the bill, even though it has now been pulled completely straight!

177. THE TALKING COIN

Props needed: A coin, a small piece of wax or tape and a long piece of black thread or fishing line.

A coin is dropped in a glass, the lights are dimmed and the coin begins to "talk" by jumping in the glass. One jump means "yes" while two jumps means "no." After the coin answers some questions, it suddenly leaps out of the glass. Everything may then be examined. Before your show, attach a long, black thread (or piece of fishing line) to the coin with a dab of wax (or some transparent tape). Hold the other end of the thread beneath the table and every time you pull on the thread the coin jumps! At the end, give the thread a hard sudden pull and the coin will jump out of the glass and will fly clear of the thread.

178. THE HANDKERCHIEF COIN VANISH

Props needed: A coin and a handkerchief.

Begin by placing a handkerchief on a table in the "diamond" position, so the points are facing up and down and side to side. Next, place a quarter in the centre of the handkerchief.

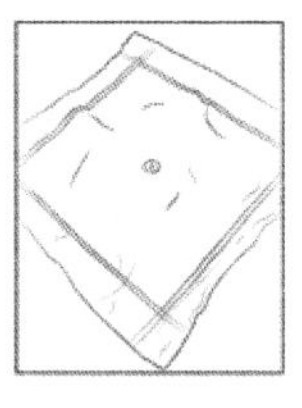

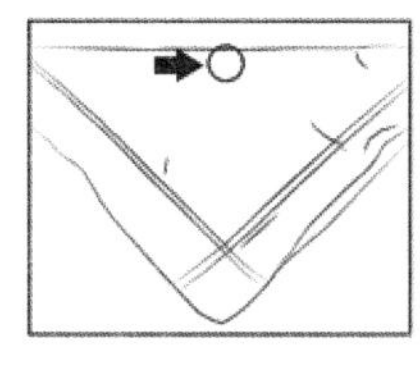

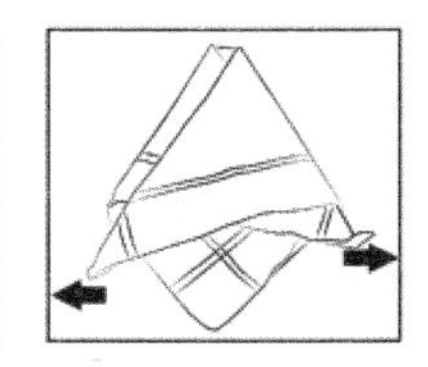

Now, fold the top corner of the handkerchief in half over the quarter. Next, fold the right-top corner diagonally across the handkerchief. Finally, fold the left-top corner diagonally across the handkerchief. Now, grab both corners and pull them away from eachother while picking the handkerchief up. This will create a small pocket which will keep the coin from falling out, making it appear that the coin has vanished!

179. PAPER TO MONEY

Props needed: A dollar bill, a piece of blank paper the size of a dollar bill and a glue stick.

For this trick, you will need a bill-sized piece of blank paper and a dollar bill. Fold both the bill and the paper into eights: fold them in half (side to side), in half again (side to side) and in half again (top to bottom). Now, unfold both the bill and the paper and using a glue stick, glue the bottom corner of the bill to the bottom corner of the paper. Fold the bill back up and you will see that it makes a tiny packet at the bottom of the paper. During your show, bring the paper out with the bill facing you and hidden behind your hand. Now, fold the paper up the way you did originally. Next, flip the paper over and unfold the bill, keeping the small packet of paper facing you. It will appear that you've turned a blank piece of paper into a real bill!

180. MULTIPLYING MONEY

Props needed: Two large coins and a small coin.

You will need two large coins and a small coin for this effect. Before you begin, hold the small coin, facing forward, between your thumb and index finger. Now, place the large coins, upright and facing sideways, between your thumb and index finger, behind the small coin. By pressing down on the large coin, you won't be able to see them behind the small coin because your fingertips will hide the extra bit of size. Begin by showing your spectators the small coin by holding it facing forward. Do not let them see it from the side or they will see the large coins! Now, show your other hand empty and form a fist around all three coins, taking them from your fingertips. Slowly open your hand to reveal the nickel and two other coins that were too big to be hidden anywhere!

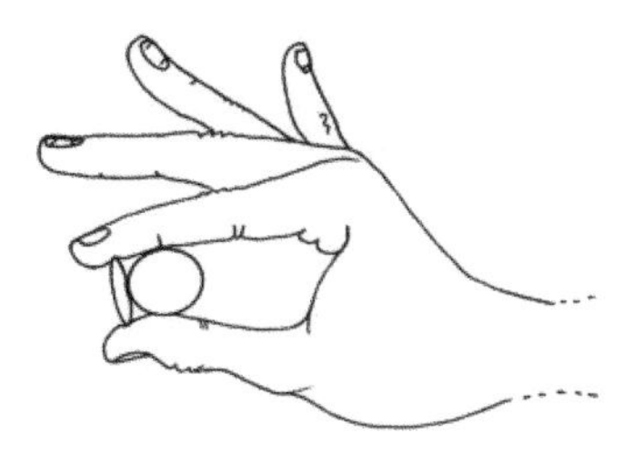

181. THE FINGER PALM VANISH

Props needed: A large coin.

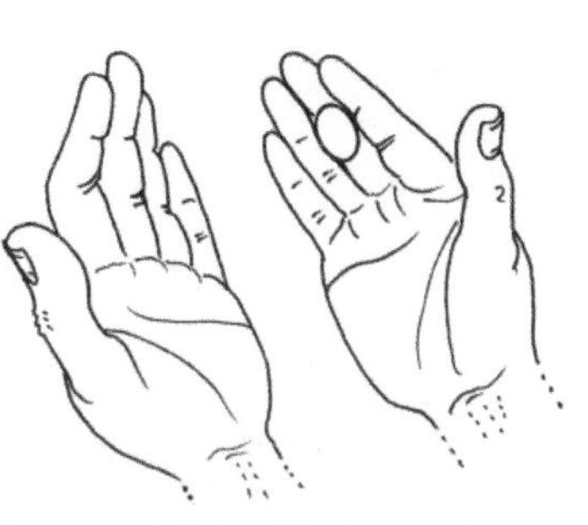

This is a classic way to vanish a coin. First, take a coin (a quarter or other large coin works well for this) and drop it into your right hand but not your palm: you are going to drop it into your fingertips. Now, you are going to let the coin rest on your middle finger while you squeeze it between your index and ring fingers. This will hold the coin in place. Now, turn your hand over as though you are dropping the coin into your left hand. Quickly close your left hand before moving your right hand away. Now, take your right hand and put it into your pocket, pretending you are getting some "magic dust." Drop the coin into your pocket. Now, pull your right hand back out and pretend to sprinkle the "magic dust" over your closed left fist. As you do this, begin to slowly open your left hand to show the coin has vanished!

182. COIN FROM EAR

Props needed: A large coin and a spectator with ears!

A classic trick of magic is vanishing a coin then reproducing it from someone's ear! Begin by doing the Finger Palm Vanish as explained above but don't do the "fairy dust" move: instead, simply open your left hand to show it empty. With your right hand, reach next to a spectator's ear and pretend to pull the coin out of their ear. Bring the coin back into their view and they will be amazed! You can also pretend to pull the coin from the air or make it reappear from just about anywhere!

183. SIGNED COIN IN ORANGE

Props needed: A small coin, a permanent marker, a knife (not too sharp!), a piece of soft wax and an orange.

Before your show, stick a small piece of soft wax (like the kind used for candy bottles) and stick it to the side of the knife. During your show, bring out the coin, orange, marker and knife and have a spectator sign the coin using the marker. Using the Finger Palm Vanish explained above, cause the coin to "disappear." While showing your left hand empty, sneakily stick the coin in your right hand to the piece of wax on the knife as you're picking it up. Be sure to keep the side of the knife with the coin on it facing toward you so the audience doesn't see it! Now, pick up the orange with your left hand and begin to cut into it. As you get about halfway through, squeeze the orange a bit so the coin dislodges from the knife and stays inside the orange. Once the knife has cut completely through the orange, separate the two halves to reveal their signed coin inside the orange!

184. ORANGE YOU GLAD I DIDN'T SAY BANANA?

Props needed: A banana, a toothpick and a deck of cards.

The night before your show, write the name of the card you plan to force on the side of a banana with a toothpick. Don't press hard — just write it like you would write with a pen on a piece of paper. The following morning, the writing will have turned brown. During your show, force a card then pretend you cannot find it in the deck. Say you must be low on potassium and ask a spectator to grab a banana out of the fruit bowl for you. Imagine their shock when they see the name of the card on the side of the banana!

185. THE VANISHING COIN

Props needed: A coin, a handkerchief and a secret helper.

You will need a secret assistant for this trick. Place a coin on your hand then cover it with a handkerchief. Walk around to all of the audience members and ask them to reach under the handkerchief and be sure the coin is still there. When you get to the last person, your secret assistant, have him reach under the handkerchief and take the coin away. Now whisk the handkerchief away and show that the coin has vanished!

186. THE PSYCHIC COIN CUP

Props needed: Four different coins, a coffee mug and a secret helper.

You will need a secret assistant for this trick. Place a coffee cup (or any cup with a handle) on the table along with a quarter, a dime, a nickel and a penny. Leave the room and instruct your audience to decide on a coin. Your secret assistant then covers the coin with the cup and hides the other coins. What your audience doesn't know is that your assistant is pointing the handle of the cup to indicate which coin is under the cup. If you imagine the space around your cup is a clock, your assistant would point the handle to the 12 position for the quarter, the 3 position for the dime, the 6 position for the nickel and the 9 position for the penny. Come back into the room and, depending on which way the handle is pointing, tell the audience which coin is under the cup!

187. MATCHBOX COIN ESCAPE

Props needed: An empty matchbox and a coin.

A coin is placed in a match box, the drawer is closed and the box is shaken to prove that the coin is still inside. When the box is opened, the coin has disappeared. The box is prepared by cutting a slit just large enough to allow a coin to slide out at one end of the drawer. The opening will not be noticed. When the box is shaken sideways, the coin will rattle but as soon as you tilt the box towards yourself, with the trick end facing you, the coin will slide out into your hand. The other hand should then take the box and lay it aside, to be opened later while you ditch the coin in your pocket.

188. THE EXTRA COIN

Props needed: Four coins and a piece of double-face tape or a loop of transparent tape.

Three coins are laid on the table. Both hands are shown empty. Your right hand sweeps the coins off the table into your left hand. When your left hand is opened it contains four coins instead of three! Before your show, attach the fourth coin to the underside of the table with a small piece of double-face tape. While your left hand is catching the three coins, use your left fingers to remove the hidden coin and allow it to drop into your left hand along with the others.

189. ATOMIC COIN

Props needed: A coin and a piece of double-face tape or a loop of transparent tape.

Tell your audience you will rub a coin so hard, you will dissolve it on an atomic level! Before your show, place a piece of double-stick tape (or a loop of tape) to the bottom of the coin. Lay it on your left palm. Cover your left palm with your right hand but in a crosswise direction. As you do this, let your right fingers push the coin over the back of your left hand and stick it to the back of your left hand. Your left hand hides the coin, so the palms of both hands may be shown. To bring the coin back, put your hands together and this time the fingers of your right hand draw the coin back from its hiding place onto your left palm.

190. THE PENETRATING COIN

Props needed: Five coins and double-face tape.

Four coins are laid on the table. With your left hand, pick up one coin and hold it beneath the table. Your right hand covers the three remaining coins. Then your left hand comes up and drops two coins on the table. Your right hand is lifted, and there are only two coins beneath it! An extra coin is used, stuck under the table with a bit of double-face tape or a loop of transparent tape. When you put your left hand under the table, simply grab the additional coin. To make one of the right-hand coins vanish is simple, but clever: one coin has a piece of double — face tape on the front of it (if you use dull coins, no one will notice). When your right hand is lifted, only two coins remain because the third coin is now stuck to your palm!

191. INTELLIGENCE DETECTOR

Props needed: A large coin and a gullible helper.

This classic "joke" trick will have your audience laughing! First take a large coin and press it hard against your forehead for about ten seconds until it sticks. Now, hold your right hand in front of your forehead and use your left hand to gently smack the back of your head until the coin falls off into your hand. Tell your audience that this is an "intellligence detector"- the more times you can smack the back of your head without the coin falling off, the more intelligent you are! Now, invite a spectator up and press the coin against his forehead hard for ten seconds. Quickly remove the coin and hide it in your hand. Because you held the coin so long and so hard against his forehead, he will still feel it as though it is stuck to his head! Now watch the audience roar with laughter as your helper smacks the back of his head over and over, convinced that it's proving him smarter!

192. HEADS OR TAILS?

Props needed: A large coin and some practice!

Lay a coin heads up in the palm of your right hand and slap the coin onto the back of your left hand. Of course the coin is now tails-up. But the next time you start with the coin heads up and it still ends up heads-up when slapped on your left hand! The trick is undetectable. If you turn your hand over naturally, the coin will always turn over with your hand but if you give the coin a tiny toss and then turn your hand quickly, only your hand will turn. The slight toss given the coin is impossible to see, as you do it while starting to turn your hand. Practice this a few times to get the timing just right!

193. COIN IN KNOT

Props needed: A coin and a cloth handkerchief.

A handkerchief is twisted in a rope-like fashion. The centre is then tied in a knot and the handkerchief is given to someone to hold. The magician makes a coin disappear but when the handkerchief is untied, the coin is discovered in the knot! The coin is vanished by using the finger-palm method and palmed in the fingers of the right hand. When the handkerchief is twisted it forms a sort of tube, sagging in the middle, the magician releases the coin and lets it slide down into this tube so that it secretly comes to the centre of the handkerchief, where it is when the knot is tied.

194. SIGNED COIN IN KNOT

Props needed: A coin, a permanent marker and a cloth handkerchief.

Since only one coin is used for the above trick, it can be immediately repeated but this time you up the ante: have a spectator draw or write anything they like on the coin before you vanish it. They will be shocked when their signed coin suddenly reappears inside the knotted handkerchief!

195. THE DOUBLE HANDKERCHIEF VANISH

Props needed: Two cloth handkerchiefs and two coins.

Combine trick # 417 and trick #430 for a cool routine! As in The Handkerchief Coin Vanish, cause a coin to vanish then, using what you learned in Coin In Knot, make a duplicate coin reappear in a knotted handkerchief! This kind of trick is called a "transposition"- where an object vanishes from one place and reappears somewhere else!

196. ANOTHER HANDKERCHIEF VANISH

Props needed: A handkerchief, a small rubber band and a coin.

A coin is pushed down into thee centre of a handkerchief but when the handkerchief is shaken, the coin has vanished! The magician holds one hand beneath the centre of the handkerchief. Around the thumb and forefinger of that hand he has a small rubber band. The coin is pushed down into the handkerchief which is pushed into the rubber band. When you release the rubber band from your fingertips, it will form a small pocket that will hold the coin in place. The handkerchief may be shaken but no trace of the coin will remain!

197. THE QUICK CLICK COIN TRICK

Props needed: A coin.

This little trick should be performed on a wooden table. The magician has a coin which he tosses from hand to hand. Finally he extends his right hand and says, "take the coin," at the same time clicking it down on the wooden table. When the person reaches to take the coin, it has disappeared! The last time you toss the coin from your left hand to your right, you only pretend to toss it. Pretend to catch the coin with your right hand and quickly put your left hand underneath the table. When your right hand pretends to lay down the coin, your left hand clicks it against the underside of table. The sound is elusive and the coin seems to be in your right hand until the moment it vanishes!

198. THE TALKING COIN

Props needed: A coin, a handkerchief, a long piece of fishing line and transparent tape.

A coin is dropped in a glass, and covered with a handkerchief. The coin begins to "talk" by jumping up and down in the glass. One jump means "yes"; two mean "no." After the coin answers some questions, it suddenly leaps out of the glass! Everything may then be examined. Before your show, attach a long piece of thin fishing line to the coin with a piece of transparent tape. You hold the other end of the thread beneath the table and every time you pull the thread the coin jumps. At the end, give the thread a hard sudden pull and the coin will jump out of the glass and fly clear of the fishing line.

199. THE OBEDIENT COIN

Props needed: Three small coins, a drinking glass and a table with a tablecloth.

A glass is set mouth-down on top of two small coins. The rim of the glass should balance on the two small coins (one on either side). Another coin is then pushed underneath the glass, between the coins. The magician states that he will cause the coin to come out from beneath the glass. He does this by scratching the tablecloth near the glass, which causes the coin to slide out from beneath the glass.

200. THE TRAVELING COIN

Props needed: Two matching coins and long pants with a cuff.

The magician borrows a coin, which he places beneath his left foot. When he raises his foot, the coin has vanished, and reappears beneath the magician's right foot. This trick should be performed seated. Two coins are used. One is secretly placed beneath the right foot. When he takes the first coin, he pretends to place it beneath his left foot but drops it in his pants cuff en route—a very simple yet effective action. Then the coin passes from the left foot to the right, both feet being raised to show the transfer!

201. COIN THROUGH NAPKIN

Props needed: A coin and a handkerchief

Hold a coin between your thumb and first finger and then cover it with a cloth napkin. Grip the napkin behind the coin with your thumb as shown. Lift up the front dangling corner of the napkin and pull it back to display the coin again. Now flick the napkin forwards and both parts of the napkin will go over the coin. It looks as if you just lifted a corner to prove the coin was there but actually the coin is now outside the napkin hidden behind it! Keeping the coin hidden behind the napkin, twist the bottom of the napkin until the twisting starts to push the coin up, making it look just as though it is magically going through the napkin! Pull the coin free and let your friends examine everything!

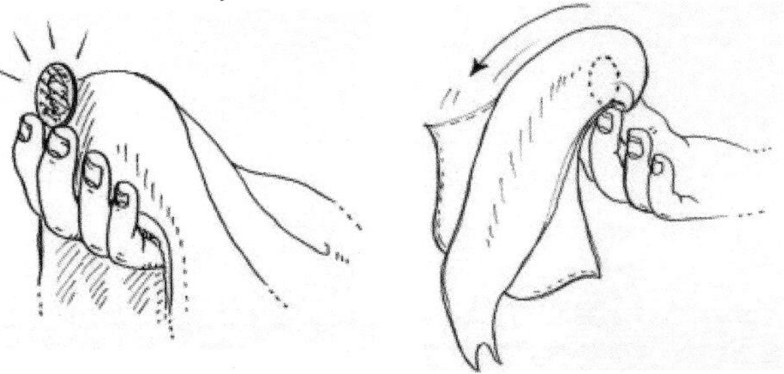

Beyond the Cube TM/MC

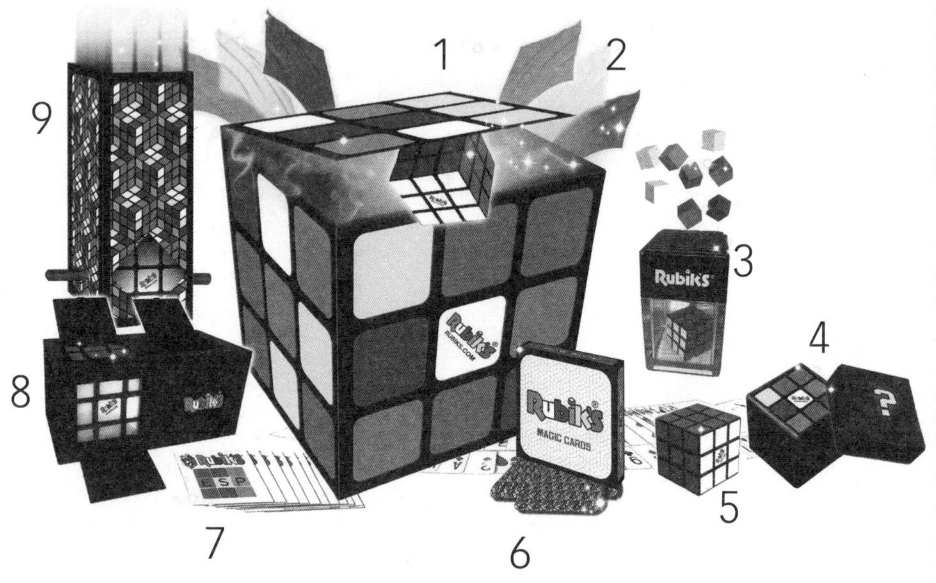

Contenu:

1. LE CUBE D'APPARITION DU RUBIK GÉANT
2. LES 6 FOULARDS RUBIK
3. LE CLONAGE DU CUBE RUBIK
(LE CONTENANT DU CUBE RUBIK, LE CUBE TRUQUÉ ET 8 CUBES MINIATURES)
4. LE CUBE RUBIK DE MENTALISME ET SA COQUILLE
5. CUBE TRUQUÉ DE TAILLE CLASSIQUE
6. LES 56 CARTES RUBIK
7. LES 11 CARTES RUBIK PES
8. LA BOITE DE CUBE RUBIK
9. LE TUBE RUBIK
10. LA VIDÉO D'INSTRUCTIONS À TÉLÉCHARGER

VIDÉO D'INSTRUCTIONS À TÉLÉCHARGER
Fantasmamagic.com/BeyondtheCube

Par l'équipe créative de Fantasma (Steve Vil. Jack Tawil, Suji Park, & Jessica Mercado).

• À conserver pour référence future. • Les couleurs et motifs peuvent varier.
• Certains tours peuvent demander l'utilisation d'objets ordinaires du quotidien.

SERVICE À LA CLIENTÈLE - FantasmaToys.com/Canada - customerservice@fantasmatoys.com

MAGIE AVEC LA BOITE DU CUBE DE MENTALISME ET SA COQUILLE

MAGIE AVEC LA BOITE À DÉ RUBIK

MAGIE AVEC LE TUBE RUBIK

MAGIE AVEC LE CLONAGE DU CUBE RUBIK

MAGIE AVEC LA BOITE D'APPARITION DU RUBIK GÉANT

MAGIE AVEC LES CARTES PES

MAGIE AVEC LES CARTES RUBIK

MAGIE AVEC OBJETS DE TOUS LES JOURS

L'ART DU MENTALISME

MAGIE DE RESTAURANT

MAGIE AVEC DE L'ARGENT

MAGIE AVEC LA BOITE DU CUBE DE MENTALISME ET SA COQUILLE

1. L'INCROYABLE CUBE RUBIK !

 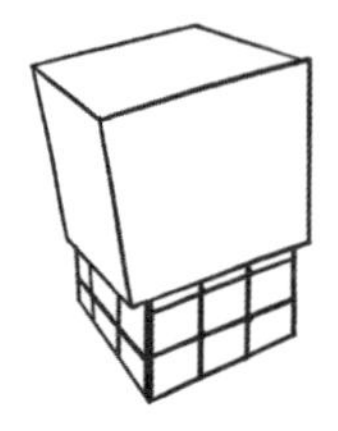 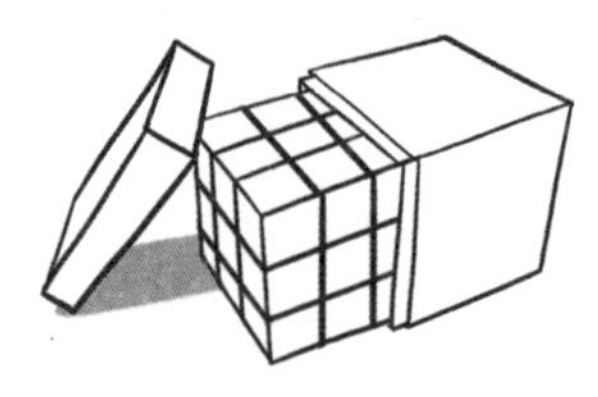

L'ensemble comprend un cube Rubik truqué, une coquille ayant l'apparence d'un cube mélangé ainsi qu'une boite noire avec couvercle. Avant le spectacle, glissez la coquille mélangée par-dessus le cube spécial. Déposez le tout sur la table de façon à ce que la coquille mélangée soit face aux spectateurs. Vos spectateurs ne voient qu'un cube Rubik mélangé d'apparence tout à fait normale. Prenez le cube délicatement en vous assurant de ne montrer que 3 côtés (il est bien important que vos spectateurs ne voient pas le côté démontrant le cube résolu). Prenez maintenant la boite et tournez-la pour que l'ouverture soit vers le bas. Glissez la boite par-dessus le cube et tournez la légèrement pour que l'ouverture soit maintenant face à vous. Couvrez la boite avec le couvercle. Secouez la boite, enlevez le couvercle et videz le contenu. La coquille restera à l'intérieur de la boite, donnant l'illusion à votre public que vous avez résolu le cube Rubik.

2. LA PRÉDICTION DU CUBE RUBIK

Vous pouvez faire bien d'autres choses avec votre cube Rubik et votre boite ! En omettant la coquille, un autre superbe tour s'offre à vous. Votre cube Rubik peut faire un autre superbe tour sans la coquille. Donnez le cube et la boite à un spectateur en lui demandant d'insérer le cube dans la boite et ce, avec n'importe quel côté (couleur) face vers le haut. Demandez-lui ensuite de poser le couvercle et de déposer le tout dans vos mains placées derrière votre dos. Dites au spectateur que vous allez tenter de lire dans ses pensées. Toujours avec les mains dans le dos, déplacez le couvercle du dessus jusqu'à l'un des côtés. Ramenez la boite en avant en vous assurant que le couvercle est vers le haut et que l'ouverture est vers vous (photo). Vous pourrez alors rapidement voir la couleur qui a été choisie par le spectateur. Prétendez lire dans les pensées avant de révéler la couleur.

MAGIE AVEC LA BOITE À DÉ RUBIK

3. LA BOITE À DÉ RUBIK

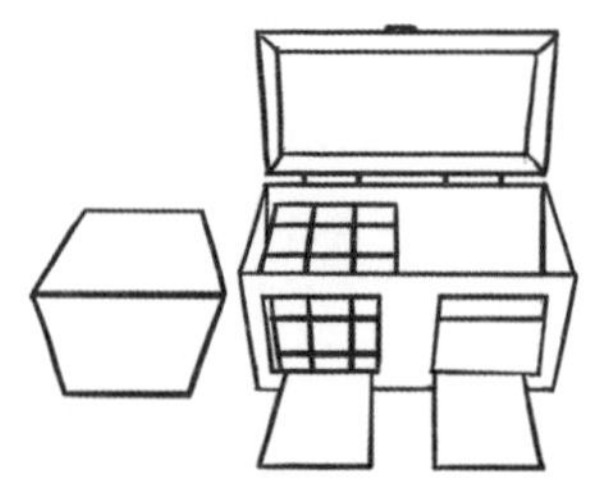

Voici une version brillante d'un tour classique utilisé par les magiciens à travers le monde. Regardons d'abord les accessoires. Premièrement, une boite avec deux portes sur le dessus et deux autres portes à l'avant. Deuxièmement, une autre coquille d'un Rubik comportant seulement trois côtés, conçue pour être déposé par-dessus le cube spécial.

Vous aurez besoin d'une boite en carton ou un chapeau assez grand pour y loger le cube. Montrez le cube avec la coquille en place en s'assurant de garder la coquille vers l'avant. Déposez le tout dans la boite (ou chapeau) en disant que plus tard, le cube apparaîtra dans cette boite (ou chapeau). Une fois l'explication terminée, sortez seulement la coquille (laissant le cube dans la boite ou le chapeau). Gardez l'ouverture de la coquille vers vous pour que personne ne voit que ce n'est pas un vrai cube.
Prenez maintenant l'accessoire avec les portes en gardant le dos de cette boite vers le public. Placez la coquille dans la boite de sorte que le bas de la coquille soit contre le bas de la boite et les coins de la coquille soient dans les coins de la boite. Fermez maintenant toutes les boites et prétendez que vous avez réussi à faire disparaitre le cube. « Prouvez » votre point en penchant la boite de l'autre côté de façon à faire croire que le cube glisse du côté opposé. Toujours en gardant le tout penché, ouvrez la porte d'en avant (où le cube était) en disant que le cube est disparu. Vos amis diront, bien entendu, que le cube est de l'autre côté. Fermez la porte et penchez maintenant le cube de l'autre côté. Ouvrez la porte (de face). Les spectateurs ont l'impression que le cube glisse d'un côté à l'autre et vous demanderont éventuellement d'ouvrir les 2 portes. Ouvrez alors la porte du dessus d'un côté et la porte de face de l'autre côté en disant que la porte des 2 côtés est ouverte. Tout le monde criera et vous demandera d'ouvrir alors les 4 portes. Vous pourrez alors les ouvrir et prouver que le cube a disparu. Montrez maintenant que le cube est apparu dans votre chapeau (ou boite).

MAGIE AVEC LE TUBE RUBIK

4. LE TUBE RUBIK

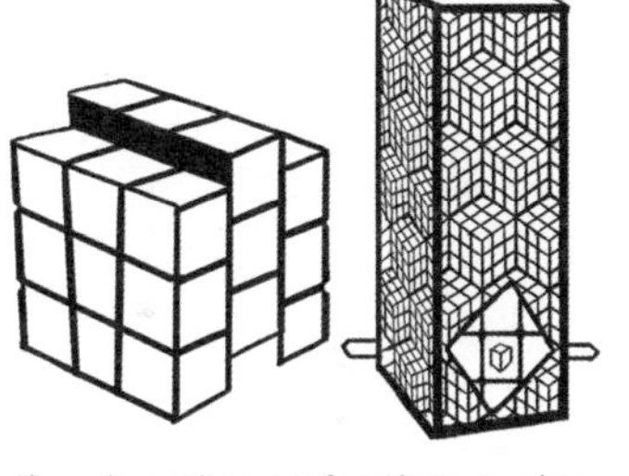

Prenez le temps de regarder votre cube Rubik et la façon dont il est fabriqué. Vous constaterez que le cube est fait de trois sections tenues ensemble à l'aide d'aimants. Collez l'un contre l'autre, vous donnerez l'impression que c'est un cube Rubik authentique. Il est même possible de tourner les côtés. Vous possédez également un long tube qui comporte deux fenêtres, une à l'avant et une à l'arrière, de petites perforations sur les côtés ainsi qu'une tige. Utilisés ensemble, ces accessoires vous permettront de faire un effet de pénétration surprenant.
Pendant votre spectacle, démontrez que le cube est normal en tournant les côtés. N'exagérez pas. Simplement quelques fois sinon le public deviendra suspicieux. Montrez maintenant le tube vide. Faites entrer la tige par les trous et affirmez au public que le cube ne peut tomber car il est retenu par la tige. Prouvez vos paroles en prenant le cube et en le laissant tomber dans le tube (assurez-vous que le logo du Rubik soit vers l'avant du tube. De cette façon, le cube frappera la tige avec un « clonk » sonore. Penchez le tube de façon à faire sortir le cube sur votre surface de travail. Passez votre main au-dessus du cube et affirmez que vous avez séparé les molécules du cube et qu'il sera donc possible pour celui-ci de passer à travers la tige. Faites entrer le cube dans le tube mais cette fois-ci, le logo être face à un des côtés. La pièce du centre du cube frappera la tige alors que les 2 côtés du cube tomberont au bas du tube. Pour le public, la tige semble avoir pénétré le cube. Vous pouvez même tourner le tube et montrer qu'on voit le même effet dans la fenêtre arrière. Enlevez maintenant la tige, ce qui fera tomber la partie centrale du cube. Grâce aux aimants, le cube se reconstituera à nouveau. Levez alors le tube pour montrer un cube 'normal' sur la table.

MAGIE AVEC LE CLONAGE DU CUBE RUBIK

5. LE CLONAGE DU CUBE

Dans votre ensemble, vous trouverez une coquille de métal qui ressemble à un petit cube Rubik, 8 petits cubes multicolores et un petit contenant transparent muni d'un couvercle noir. Pour vous préparer, déposez délicatement les 8 petits cubes dans la coquille de métal. Lorsque vous déposez la coquille ouverture vers le bas, le public ne voit qu'un petit cube Rubik normal. Commencez votre spectacle avec la coquille/cubes sur la table (ouverture vers le bas). Montrez ensuite le contenant transparent ainsi que le couvercle. Prenez maintenant la coquille avec les cubes de la façon suivante : inclinez la coquille légèrement vers l'avant tout en mettant votre pouce sous les petits cubes pour empêcher qu'ils tombent. Agrippez ensuite la coquille entre vos doigts et votre pouce. Vous pouvez montrer le cube de presque tous les côtés. Prenez le contenant en gardant l'ouverture vers les spectateurs. Entrez la coquille et les cubes dans l'ouverture en vous assurant de ne pas exposer le dessous de la coquille. Repositionnez le contenant ouverture vers le haut et mettez le couvercle. Secouez le contenant vers le haut. En ce faisant, la coquille restera bien collée à l'intérieur du couvercle grâce aux aimants, tandis que les petits cubes voleront en éclats. Pour le public, le cube semble avoir explosé en plusieurs petits cubes. Retirez le couvercle et déposez-le sur la table (ouverture vers le bas). Versez les cubes sur la table.

6. LE BALL-O-CUBE

Plutôt que de mettre les cubes dans la coquille, vous pouvez mettre d'autres objets. Vous pouvez, par exemple, y insérer une petite balle. Lorsque vous secouerez le contenant de bas en haut, le cube se transformera en balle qui rebondira partout. Cette illusion peut même sembler plus incroyable que le CLONAGE DU CUBE car il y a eu modification de forme, et de matière.

7. LE CUBE ET PIÈCE

Prenez plusieurs pièces de monnaie et déposez-les dans votre coquille. Demandez aux spectateurs combien vaut un petit cube. Sans même leur donner le temps de répondre, secouez le cube de haut en bas. Le public sera surpris de voir le contenant se remplir de pièces de monnaie. Vous serez agréablement surpris de constater la réaction de vos spectateurs.

8. LE CUBE ET DÉ

Prenez un dé et déposez-le dans la coquille. Secouez le tout et laisser le public apprécier le fait que le cube s'est transformé en dé. Si vous possédez 2 autres dés, le prochain effet est tout indiqué.

9. LE DÉ MENTAL

Une fois le cube transformé en dé, prenez vos deux autres dés pour créer un effet de mentalisme. Avant votre spectacle, écrivez le nombre « 21 » sur un bout de papier et déposez-le dans votre poche. Demandez à un spectateur de jeter les 3 dés sur la table pour prouver qu'ils sont normaux (elle peut même utiliser le contenant). Demandez-lui de rouler les dés une autre fois et d'additionner la somme des dés ainsi que la somme du dessous des dés. La somme sera TOUJOURS 21. Prenez alors votre prédiction pour prouver que vous aviez raison.

10. LE TÉLÉPHONE PSYCHIQUE

Pour l'effet précédent, vous pourriez être de connivence avec un de vos amis de la façon suivante. Dites-lui qu'à chaque fois que quelqu'un l'appelle et demande pour L'INCROYABLE ERNO, de répondre : « BONJOUR, LE TOTAL DE VOS DÉS EST 21 ». Avec cette illusion, vous demandez au spectateur d'appeler l'incroyable Erno, au lieu de produire votre prédiction en papier. Très puissant et peut être fait n'importe où. Votre ami saura quoi faire à chaque fois que quelqu'un l'appellera en demandant pour l'incroyable Erno.

11. LE CUBE À TRAVERS LA TABLE

Ce tour est parfait lorsque vous êtes assis à une table. Dites à vos amis que vous allez faire passer le cube (en fait la coquille) à travers la table. Placez le cube sur la table. Déposez par-dessus le contenant transparent. Couvrez maintenant le contenant d'une feuille de papier journal. Pressez la feuille pour qu'elle prenne la forme du contentant. D'une main tapez le dessus du contenant alors que de l'autre, vous soulevez le contenant (avec le journal) et le dirigez légèrement au-dessus de vos cuisses tout en regardant le cube qui est toujours sur la table. Dites à votre auditoire que vous n'avez pas réussi votre tour, ce qui évident car le cube est toujours sous leurs yeux. Alors que tout le monde regarde le cube, relâchez juste assez de pression pour faire tomber le contenant sur vos cuisses. Comme le papier a la même forme que le contenant, personne ne s'imaginera que le contenant a disparu. Déplacez le papier journal au-dessus du cube et écrasez-le de votre main. Sortez le contenant, comme s'il avait passé à travers la table et mentionnez que vous ne connaissez pas votre propre force

MAGIE AVEC LA BOITE D'APPARITION DU RUBIK GÉANT

12. L'ILLUSION DU CUBE ET DU RUBIK

Commencez par déplier le couvercle de la boite de façon à ce qu'il soit vers l'extérieur de la boite. Ouvrez la boite pour lui donner l'apparence d'un cube. Sous la boite, vous trouverez 3 rabats avec des ailerons pour accrocher. Reliez tous les rabats et ailerons pour préserver la forme du cube. Ouvrez la boite par le dessous et dépliez la section qui deviendra votre compartiment secret (pour produire des objets). Vous devrez tourner et déplier, pratiquement bout pour bout. Vous retrouverez d'autres ailerons sur le « mur » arrière. Appuyez le compartiment secret contre le mur arrière (donc contre les 2 ailerons). Un aileron se trouve de chaque côté du fond du compartiment secret. Insérez-les dans leurs trous respectifs.

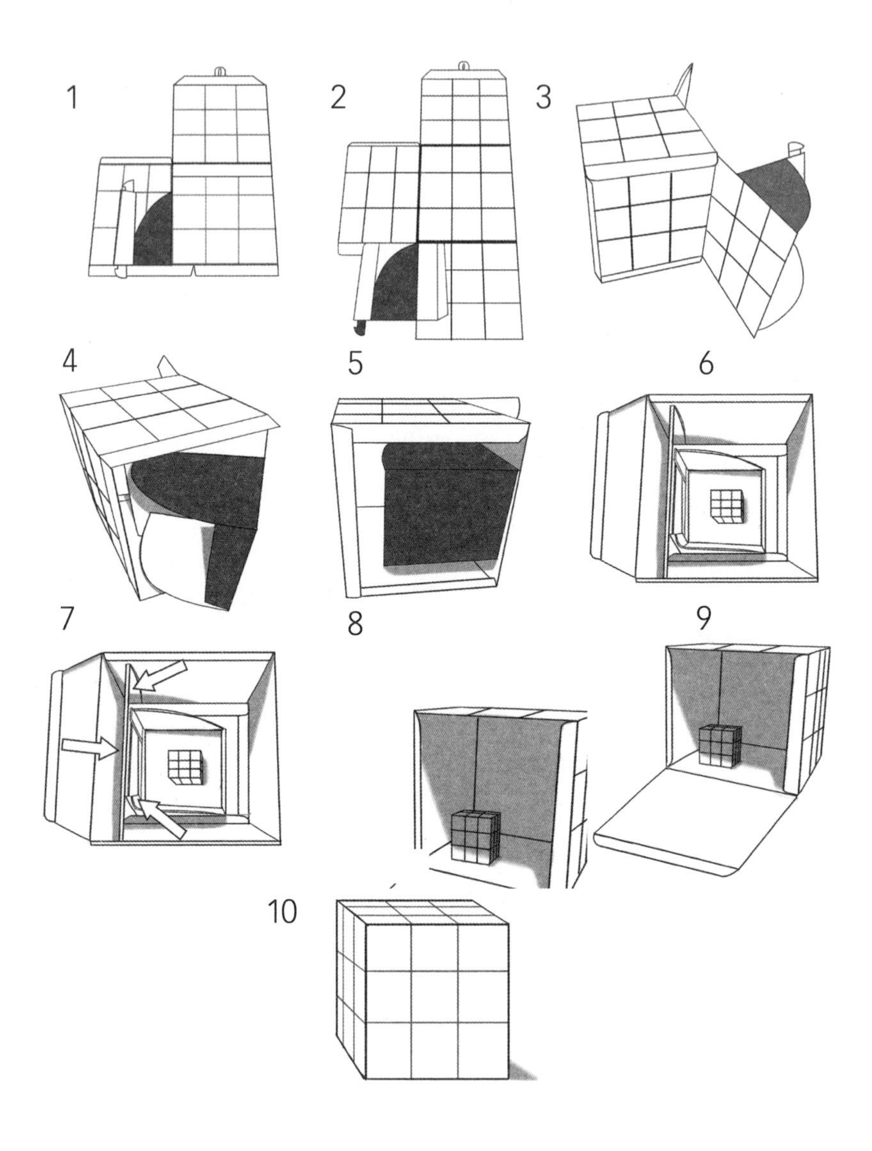

13. COMMENT PERFORMER UNE PRODUCTION INCROYABLE !

Avant votre spectacle, déposez votre cube spécial dans le compartiment secret. Placez un foulard dans la boite (à l'extérieur du compartiment secret). Tournez la boite vers vos spectateurs et inclinez-la vers eux. Le compartiment secret demeure sur la table. Ouvrez la boite pour montrer qu'elle est vide sauf pour un ou deux foulards. Vous avez le choix de les laisser à l'intérieur ou de les sortir. Fermez le couvercle et inclinez la boite vers vous (le couvercle se retrouvera vers le haut). Ouvrez le couvercle à nouveau et montrez que les foulards se sont transformés en cube.

14. PRODUCTIONS MULTIPLES

Vous pouvez utiliser cette boite pour un effet cocasse tout au long de votre spectacle. Par exemple, tous vos accessoires pourraient être cachés dans votre compartiment secret et vous pouvez les faire apparaître à votre guise. Montrez la boite vide et faites apparaître votre premier accessoire. Après ce tour, montrez la boite vide de nouveau et faites apparaître votre deuxième accessoire. Pourquoi ne pas répéter cette illusion pour chaque accessoire dont vous avez besoin pour un tour ?

15. UNE BELLE FINALE !

À la fin de votre spectacle, vous pouvez récupérer vos accessoires et les remettre dans la boite. Faites alors disparaitre le tout pour une finale épatante !

16.UNE AUTRE BELLE FINALE !

Déposez quelques friandises dans le compartiments secret de votre coffre. À la fin de votre spectacle, faites apparaître les friandises et partagez-les avec vos spectateurs. Vous serez le magicien le plus populaire en ville !

17. ORIGANIMO

Mettez un animal en peluche dans votre coffre (évidemment, n'utilisez pas un animal vivant). Montrez que votre coffre est vide et expliquez que vous êtes un expert en origami. Prenez un mouchoir et dites que vous allez en faire un animal. Déchirez le mouchoir et déposez-le dans la boite. Faites apparaître votre animal en peluche et acceptez les applaudissements.

18. DÉCHIRÉ ET RECONSTITUÉ

Votre coffre peut également être utilisé pour substituer des objets. Ces objets doivent par contre être d'une taille pouvant s'insérer dans la section entre le compartiment secret et la paroi du coffre. Munissez-vous de 2 pages de journal identiques et insérez-en une dans l'espace entre le compartiment secret et la paroi du coffre. Durant votre spectacle, ouvrez le coffre, sortez-en la page du journal et montrez le coffre vide aux spectateurs. Refermez le coffre, déchirez la page et déposer les morceaux de papier dans le coffre. D'un geste magique, retirez la seconde page, montrant à vos spectateurs que vous avez réussi l'impossible !

19. DÉCHIRÉ ET... RECONSTITUÉ ?

Déchirez votre page et recollez-la avec du ruban noir de façon très apparente. Déposez la page dans le compartiment et une feuille identique dans la section avant. Ouvrez votre coffre et sortez la feuille. Comme lors du tour précédent, vous déchirez le journal et déposez les morceaux dans le coffre. Affirmez que vous le reconstituerez en y ajoutant du ruban noir dans le coffre. Sortez maintenant le papier journal tout recollé avec le ruban. Des éclats de rire suivront. Terminez en disant « est-ce qu'il y une meilleure façon de le faire ? »

MAGIE AVEC LES CARTES PES

20. LES CARTES RUBIK PES

Les cartes PES sont uniques : vous trouverez une carte (la carte-clé) avec ses 9 couleurs (rouge, orange, vert, bleu, blanc, mauve, noir et rose) et 10 autres cartes avec une configuration différentes des couleurs mentionnées ainsi qu'un gros trou où 2 couleurs sont manquantes. Vous pouvez, avec ces cartes, faire de la lecture de pensée. Montrez d'abord la carte-clé. Demandez ensuite à un spectateur de choisir une couleur sans la dévoiler. Prenez ensuite les 10 autres cartes et montrez-les au spectateur en lui demandant si la couleur à laquelle il pense se trouve sur chaque carte. Faites une pile avec les cartes « oui » et une autre avec les cartes « non ». Prenez la pile des « oui » et déposez-la sur la carte-clé. Cette pile doit vous faire face et non être face au spectateur. En mettant la pile de « oui » sur la carte-clé, une ouverture se crée où seule une couleur sera visible. C'est bien évidement la couleur choisie. Après avoir mémorisé la couleur, déposez la pile des « non » sur la carte-clé. Annoncez maintenant la couleur choisie par le spectateur, au grand étonnement de la foule.

1

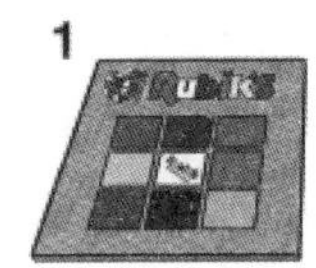

2

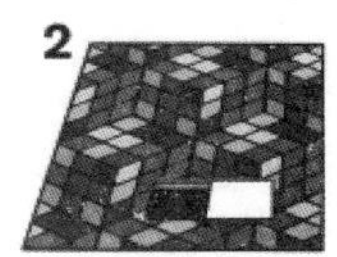

MAGIE AVEC LES CARTES RUBIK

21. LES CARTES RUBIK

Vos cartes ont une marque spéciale qui vous permet de connaître l'identité d'une carte avec un seul regard au dos de chaque carte. L'explication du marquage des cartes est à l'endos du manuel mais en voici une brève explication. Chaque couleur est représentée par une couleur différente au dos de la carte. Bleu = pique, vert = trèfle, rouge = cœur, orange = carreau. Dans le coin inférieur gauche, vous retrouverez une rangée de carrés jaunes en groupes de 3. La valeur de la carte est déterminée par la localisation de la couleur dans la rangée. Exemple : si le premier carré dans la rangée jaune est bleu, la carte est donc l'as de pique. Si le carré bleu était en deuxième position, la carte serait le 2 de pique. Les 3 derniers carrés (onzième, douzième et treizième positions) représentent le valet, la dame et le roi

22. C'EST VOTRE CARTE ?

La façon la plus facile d'utiliser le paquet est de trouver une carte. Malgré que ce tour semble très simple, vos spectateurs seront ébahis par votre talent. Faites choisir une carte et au même moment que le spectateur la retire du paquet, observez bien la petite marque. Laissez le spectateur bien mélanger le paquet et reprenez-le. Étalez les cartes devant vous, choisissez rapidement la carte que vous avez mémorisé et montrez-la au public.

23. VISION EXTRAORDINAIRE

Faites choisir une carte et demandez au spectateur de la couvrir de ses mains. N'oubliez pas de lire la marque avant qu'il la couvre. Prétendez être doué d'une vision surhumaine. Regardez chaque carte du paquet en disant que vous calculez quelle carte est manquante. Effectuez cette tâche le plus rapidement possible. Refermez le jeu et nommez la carte, prouvant à tous que votre vision est vraiment extraordinaire.

24. LECTURE DE PENSÉE

Le succès de cet effet repose sur vos talents d'acteur. Une carte est choisie et mélangée dans le paquet. Demandez au spectateur de se concentrer sur la carte. Dévoilez la carte petit à petit en commençant par affirmez si elle est rouge ou noire, pour ensuite révéler la couleur et finalement la valeur. Prétendez faire un immense effort de concentration pour un effet incroyable.

25. LECTURE DE PENSÉE EXTRÊME

Vous pouvez augmenter l'enjeu en faisant choisir trois cartes. Replacez deux des cartes dans le paquet alors que vous déposez la troisième dans la poche du spectateur. Devinez lentement les deux premières cartes et annoncez que la troisième s'annonce beaucoup plus difficile. Évidemment, vous savez qu'elle n'est pas plus difficile, mais vos talents d'acteur font la différence. La présentation que vous utiliserez est plus importante que le tour lui-même. Quand vous aurez finalement deviné la troisième carte, prenez une grande respiration et dites : « C'était très difficile ».

26. TOUTE UNE COÏNCIDENCE

Séparez votre paquet en deux et donnez une des deux moitiés à un spectateur. Demandez-lui de prendre une carte dans sa moitié et de la mémoriser. Assurez-vous d'être capable de lire la marque sur la carte. Demandez-lui ensuite de remettre sa carte dans votre propre moitié. Alors que vous mélangez, dites : « Comme vous m'avez donné une carte, c'est bien normal que je vous en donne une à mon tour ». Prenez la carte qu'il a choisie et redonnez-lui. Demandez au spectateur quelle était sa carte. Étalez ensuite votre moitié sur la table. Sa carte n'est évidemment pas là. Montrez que vous lui avez redonné sa propre carte.

27. LES BONNES PAIRES

Donnez à un spectateur six cartes, de l'as au 6 de cœur. Alors qu'elle les brasse, sortez les 6 cartes de l'as au 6 de pique et faites un éventail avec les faces vers vous. Demandez au spectateur de choisir un de ses 6 cartes face vers le bas sur la table. Concentrez-vous et déposez la carte jumelle sur cette carte. Demandez au spectateur de déposer une autre carte face vers le bas à côté de l'autre paire et une fois de plus, déposez la carte jumelle par-dessus. Répétez ces actions pour les quatre autres cartes. Affirmez finalement : « je ne suis pas certain à 100%, mais j'ai un bon sentiment ». Tournez les paires, démontrant une coïncidence parfaite.

28. VOUS POUVEZ LE FAIRE

C'est maintenant au tour de votre spectateur de faire coïncider les paires. En plus d'utiliser les marques, vous utiliserez un principe appelé « le système un coup d'avance ». Une fois de plus, retirez 6 cartes, de l'as au 6 de cœur ainsi que de l'as au 6 de pique.

Ajoutez secrètement une carte à votre petit paquet. Dites : « je vous ai prouvé mon talent, voyons voir le vôtre maintenant ». Déposez une carte sur la table et demandez au spectateur de mettre une des cartes par-dessus. Prenez le temps de lire le marquage et déposez la carte jumelle de celle-ci par-dessus. Recommencez ce stratagème jusqu'à ce que toutes les cartes soient dans cette pile. La dernière carte sera la carte jumelle de celle en dessous de la pile, la première que vous avez déposée, ce qui vous demandera un léger ajustement. Soulevez la pile de cartes et, tout en prenant celle du dessus, dites : « prenez les cartes et déposez-les face vers le haut une à une sur la table ». Utilisez la carte que vous tenez pour pointer vers la table. Remettez la carte dans le paquet, mais en dessous plutôt que sur le dessus. Donnez le paquet au spectateur et vous verrez 6 paires parfaites prouvant qu'eux aussi ont des pouvoirs.

29. LE FRUIT DU HASARD

Parfois en performant l'effet précédent, le spectateur, à son insu, déposera la carte jumelle de votre propre carte. Lorsque cette superbe coïncidence se produit, mettez cette paire à l'écart en disant « j'ai un bon pressentiment, mettons cette paire de côté ». Continuez le numéro tel que décrit précédemment. Au moment de conclure, tournez la première paire et dites : « Une paire parfaite, mais ce n'est qu'un début ». Comme auparavant, demandez-leur de distribuer le reste des cartes (en faisant votre ajustement). Il se peut que la deuxième paire soit également un match parfait. Si c'est le cas, mettez-la de côté et dites : « Wow, de mieux en mieux ». Plus rarement, vous aurez cinq paires parfaites. Si vous avez cette chance inouïe, clamez que c'est un réel miracle !

30. ROUGE ET NOIR

Donnez le paquet à un spectateur et demandez-lui de prendre une carte rouge et une noire et de les déposer côte-à-côte sur la table (face vers le haut). Prétendez pouvoir deviner si une carte est rouge ou noire. Demandez alors au spectateur de tenir une carte vers le bas devant vous. Touchez légèrement la carte et annoncez sa couleur. Demandez-lui de la déposer face vers le bas sur la carte correspondante sur la table. Dites : « Nous allons vérifier si j'ai raison dans un instant ». Répétez avec le reste du paquet. « Ce serait un petit miracle si j'avais réussi à séparer le paquet en deux parties égales, mais ce n'est rien à côté de ce qui suit ». Tournez les deux piles et montrez que vous avez réussi à diviser le paquet en deux moitiés : une rouge et une noire. Vous pouvez raccourcir ce tour en n'utilisant que la moitié du paquet

31. MÊME LES COULEURS

Pour un effet encore plus surprenant, ajoutez un niveau de difficulté. Affirmez à vos spectateurs que vous pouvez séparer le paquet en quatre couleurs. Pour plus d'effet, brassez le paquet de nouveau. Répétez toutes les actions de l'effet précédent en séparant les cœurs des carreaux. Faites la même chose avec les cartes noires. Vous aurez alors quatre piles sur la table. Tournez ces quatre piles pour montrer que vous avez réussi. Terminez en disant : « une chance que j'utilise mes pouvoirs pour le bien ! ».

32. PLACEMENT PARFAIT

Demandez au spectateur de déposer cinq cartes en une seule rangée sur la table. Étudiez attentivement les cartes et dites : « ce n'est pas une rangée parfaite, mais c'est tout de même assez proche ». Poursuivez : « lorsque je me retournerai, déplacez deux des cartes ». Ne regardez pas pendant que le spectateur déplace les deux cartes. Une fois cette action accomplie, affirmez en les pointant que vous savez quelles cartes ont été déplacées. Évidemment, les marques au dos des cartes vous indiquent facilement quelles cartes ont été déplacées. Vous pouvez répéter cet effet plusieurs fois mais nous vous recommandons de ne pas l'utiliser plus de trois fois. Après tout, inutile de faire rager vos spectateurs !

33. LA CARTE-CLÉ (DESSUS)

Voici une façon très subtile d'utiliser votre jeu marqué. Mélangez le jeu, déposez-le sur la table et mémorisez la carte du dessus. Demandez à un spectateur de penser à une carte sans vous la dévoiler. Retournez-vous, demandez au spectateur de retirer la carte et de la déposer sur le dessus du paquet. Faites ensuite couper le paquet. Dites aux spectateurs qu'il est impossible pour vous de connaître l'identité de la carte. Pour une des rares fois, cet énoncé est vrai. Prenez le paquet et prétendez que vous vous concentrez intensément, pour ensuite étaler les cartes. Vous ne connaissez pas la carte mais vous connaissez celle juste à côté (la carte du dessus). La carte choisie sera la carte à la gauche de celle-ci.

34. LA CARTE-CLÉ (DESSOUS)

Prenez votre paquet et mémorisez la carte sous le paquet. Cette carte est maintenant votre carte-clé. Étalez les cartes et demandez à un spectateur de prendre une carte. Dites au spectateur de mémoriser sa carte et de la remettre sur le paquet. Coupez le paquet (ce qui veut dire de prendre environ la moitié des cartes du dessous et les mettre sur le dessus). Ceci aura comme effet de positionner votre carte-clé directement au-dessus de la carte choisie. Tournez les cartes face vers le haut. Il ne vous restera qu'à localiser la carte-clé. La carte choisie sera directement à droite de votre carte-clé.

35. UNE BONNE IMPRESSION

Le principe de la carte-clé s'exprime particulièrement bien en faisant choisir une carte à un volontaire pour ensuite la remettre dans le paquet. Dites : « Comme tout bon détective, je trouverai votre carte lorsque j'y verrai vos empreintes digitales » ou bien « Je trouverai votre carte grâce à mon incroyable odorat ! ». Prétendez chercher la carte méticuleusement (vous pouvez même en sentir une ou deux) avant de clamer « Cette carte respire votre parfum ! ». Montrez-la, car c'est bien évidemment la bonne carte. L'ajout de présentations animées de la sorte aidera à créer une bonne impression.

36. LES POLICIERS ATTRAPENT LES VOLEURS

Une fois de plus, le principe de la carte-clé est utilisée de façon magistrale. Une carte est sélectionnée et « perdue » dans le paquet. Vous affirmez alors devoir aller à la recherche de deux policiers. Retirez les deux valets noirs et déposez-les sur la table. Du même coup, repérez la carte-clé et coupez le paquet de façon à ce que la carte-clé soit en dessous du paquet (laissant la sélection sur le dessus). Vous devez maintenant mettre le paquet soit sous la table ou dans votre dos et prendre les valets. Affirmez au public que vous remettez les valets face vers le haut dans le paquet. En réalité, vous mettrez un valet en 2ième position et l'autre sur le dessus (la carte choisie sera donc entre les 2 valets). Vous faites une coupe complète avant de ramener le paquet. Étalez le paquet sur la table pour montrer la carte entre les valets et attendez que le spectateur confirme l'identité de sa carte.

37. CE TOUR PREND UN AN, UN MOIS ET UNE SEMAINE

Tournez la carte sous le paquet face vers le haut. Faites choisir une carte en vous assurant de ne pas montrer que la carte du dessous est retournée. Faites replacer la sélection sur le dessus du jeu et coupez le jeu. Étalez les cartes et « remarquez » la carte renversée. Coupez le jeu à cet endroit et remettez la carte renversée à l'endroit. La carte choisie sera la deuxième du dessus. Demandez aux spectateurs le nombre de semaines dans une année. Évidemment la réponse sera 52. Déposez cinq cartes, une à la fois dans une pile, et ensuite deux dans une autre pile. Déposez maintenant les 2 cartes sur la pile de 5 cartes pour ensuite prendre les 7 cartes et les remettre sur le paquet. Demandez ensuite aux spectateurs le nombre de mois dans une année. Après leur réponse, prendre une carte à la fois du paquet et les déposez en une pile de 12, que vous déposerez ensuite sur le paquet. Finalement, demandez aux spectateurs le nombre de jours dans une semaine. Après la réponse, distribuez 7 cartes sur la table (toujours une à une) et déposez cette pile sur le paquet. Tournez la première carte du dessus du paquet. C'est la carte choisie.

38. PERDUE

Une autre belle façon d'utiliser le principe de la carte-clé est de prétendre avoir manqué le tour. Faites choisir une carte et « perdez-la » dans le jeu. Dites : « je vais distribuer les cartes une à une et face vers le haut en espérant trouver votre carte ». Alors que vous distribuez les cartes, soyez attentif pour localiser la carte-clé. Vous savez que la prochaine sera la carte choisie mais n'arrêtez pas de distribuer, continuer à déposer des cartes (3-4 cartes après la carte choisie). Dites : « la prochaine carte que je tournerai est votre carte ». Comme tout le monde a déjà vu la carte passer, les gens croiront que vous vous êtes trompé. Mais ils seront épatés quand vous irez chercher la bonne carte dans la rangée de cartes déjà tournées.

39. ÉCOUTEZ MA VOIX

Voici une façon amusante d'utiliser le principe de la carte-clé. Une fois la carte choisie et remise dans le jeu, dites : « Nous allons voir si vous pouvez contrôler votre voix ». Retournez-vous (pour ne pas voir la table) et demandez au spectateur de distribuer les cartes une à une sur la table, face vers le haut, en nommant les cartes. Prétendez que qu'uniquement par le timbre de sa voix, vous êtes en mesure de trouver la carte. Évidemment, attendez qu'il nomme la carte-clé. La prochaine sera la bonne.

40. SCANNER

Commencez avec les 4 as sur le dessus du jeu et remettez le paquet à un spectateur. Demandez-lui de distribuer les cartes une à une sur la table en une seule pile. Indiquez qu'elle peut arrêter où elle veut mais qu'elle doit avoir plus de 10 cartes. Une fois qu'elle a terminé, demandez-lui de prendre la pile et d'en faire 4 piles en distribuant les cartes une à une. Dites : « je ne pouvais pas prédire combien de cartes vous alliez distribuer, alors expliquez-moi ceci ». Demandez au spectateur de tourner la carte du dessus de chaque pile. Évidemment, ce seront les 4 as.

41. LA RÉPLIQUE

Sortez du paquet les 4 rois, les 4 dames, les 4 valets et les 4 as. Débutez 4 piles différentes avec 4 as, face vers le haut. Déposez un roi sur chaque as, pour ensuite poursuivre avec les dames et les valets. Combinez les 4 piles ensemble pour n'en faire qu'une. Coupez le paquet quelques fois. En distribuant les cartes une à une, faites 4 piles. Tournez chaque pile face vers le haut. Chaque pile sera constituée d'un as, un roi, une dame et un valet.

42. LES AS SUR LE DESSUS

Avant votre spectacle, enlevez les 4 as et mettez-les dans votre poche. Durant votre spectacle, demandez à un spectateur de mélanger les cartes. Une fois terminé, reprenez le jeu et glissez-le dans votre poche (sous les as) en disant que vous allez faire un tour incroyable. Ressortez le jeu, faites un geste magique et montrez que les as sont sur le dessus.

43. LA CARTE DOUBLE-DOS

Vous remarquerez que le paquet Dextérité vient également avec une carte double-dos. En mettant cette carte sous le paquet, vous réaliserez des effets fantastiques. Étalez d'abord les cartes face vers le bas et demandez à un spectateur de choisir une carte. Alors que tous les regards sont tournés vers la carte choisie, tournez le paquet face vers le haut. Grâce à la carte double-dos, le paquet semble normal. Prenez la carte choisie et insérez-la dans le jeu en vous assurant de garder le paquet bien en place. Dites que vous retrouverez la carte avec le paquet dans votre dos. Une fois le paquet dans votre dos, retournez simplement le paquet de l'autre côté. Déposez maintenant le paquet sur la table et étalez les cartes pour montrer que la carte choisie est renversée.

44. SUPER DOUBLE-DOS

Créez un effet encore plus grandiose en faisant choisir plusieurs cartes. Vous pourriez en faire choisir de 10 à 15 mais pour un début, commencez avec 3. Répétez les étapes du tour précédent mais places les 3 cartes à des endroits différents du paquet. Expliquez au public qu'une carte c'est déjà bien difficile à trouver mais que 3 c'est beaucoup plus compliqué. Une fois le paquet dans le dos et retourné, ramenez-le vers l'avant, déposez-le sur la table et dites : « Non seulement ai-je retrouvé chaque carte mais en plus, je les ai retournées face vers le haut dans le paquet ». Étalez le paquet, montrant les cartes choisies, et attendez les applaudissements.

45. LE PAQUET ENTÊTÉ

Commencez avec la carte double-dos sur le dessus du jeu. Étalez les cartes face vers le bas. Expliquez que vous avez entre les mains un paquet très entêté car à chaque fois que vous mettez une carte face vers le haut, elle se remet face vers le bas d<elle-même. Demandez à un spectateur de prendre la carte du dessus sans la retourner. Étalez maintenant les cartes, face vers le haut cette fois-ci, et demandez au spectateur de replacer sa carte où il le veut. Refermez le jeu et retournez-le à nouveau face vers le bas. Étalez une dernière fois le paquet et montrez qu'il n'y a pas de carte face vers le haut. Sa carte s'est retournée d'elle-même

46. LA CARTE À TRAVERS LE FOULARD

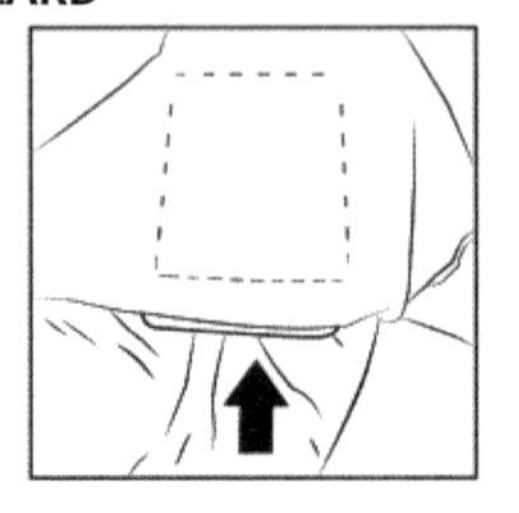

Faites choisir une carte par le spectateur et replacez cette dernière sur le dessus du jeu. En tenant le paquet dans votre main gauche, couvrez-le d'un foulard. Avec votre main droite, prenez le paquet au complet (toujours sous le foulard) à l'exception de la carte du dessus (la carte choisie) de façon discrète. Placez le paquet au-dessus du foulard dans votre main gauche, directement au-dessus de la carte choisie. Pliez la partie du foulard de l'arrière vers l'avant (par-dessus le paquet). Vous apercevrez le bord de la carte qui vous fera face. Pliez le reste du foulard vers le bas autour du paquet et de la carte. Vous verrez que le paquet est complètement couvert du foulard mais que la carte peut aisément se libérer. Prenez le foulard par les pointes; le paquet est donc maintenant à l'intérieur d'un petit baluchon. La carte restera en place. Agrippez la carte et sortez-la doucement. Donnez le tout pour vérification. Les spectateurs constateront que le paquet est bel et bien dans le foulard.

47. D'UN CÔTÉ COMME DE L'AUTRE

Certains paquets de cartes ont un dos unidirectionnel : c'est-à-dire que plutôt que d'avoir un dos symétrique, le dos est asymétrique (une seule image plutôt qu'une image reproduite 2 fois). Votre paquet est spécial car la ligne jaune est uniquement présente du côté gauche. Commencez en vous assurant que chaque carte est orientée de la même façon. Pendant votre spectacle, étalez les cartes face vers le bas et demandez à un spectateur d'en choisir une. Reprenez les cartes et tournez-les dans l'autre sens (toujours face vers le bas). Demandez au spectateur d'y remettre sa carte. Étalez les cartes dans vos mains avec le dos face à vous. Vous verrez automatiquement la carte choisie car elle sera la seule qui aura le dos dans la direction opposée.

48. LE BONNETEAU À 2 CARTES

Examinez attentivement vos cartes spéciales. L'une d'entre elles est une carte à double-dos et l'autre est une carte double-face. Évidemment, votre public n'est pas au courant de l'existence de ces cartes truquées. Déposez la carte double-face par-dessus la carte double-dos. Déplacez légèrement la carte du dessus (double-face) de façon à voir le coin de la carte inférieure (comme un éventail de cartes). Tenez les 2 cartes avec le pouce au-dessus et l'index en-dessous (et vers le centre). Montrez les 2 cartes et dans l'action de vouloir montrer les cartes du dessous, tournez votre main paume vers

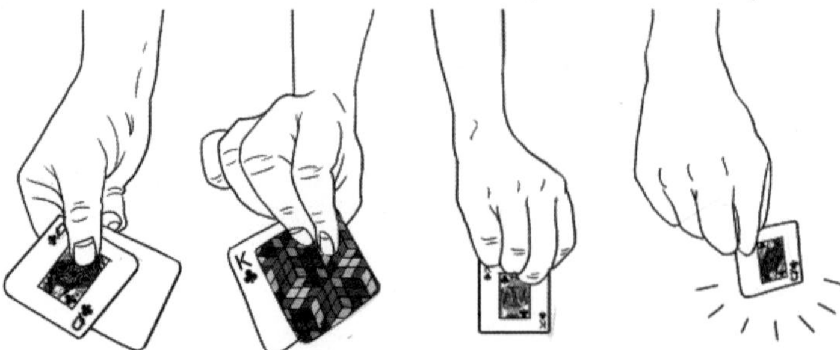

le bas. Au même moment, faites glisser la carte du dessus vers la gauche. Lorsque votre paume est orientée vers le bas, les gens voient le second côté de la carte double-face alors qu'ils croient voir la seconde carte. Retournez la paume vers le haut en glissant cette-fois-ci la carte vers la droite. Pratiquez plusieurs fois pour rendre le mouvement fluide. Prenez la carte du dessus (double-face), montrez-la et mettez-la dans votre dos. Demandez alors à vos spectateurs quelle est la carte restante. Évidemment, ils diront tous le nom de la seconde carte. Vous allez retourner la carte dans votre dos et la ramener devant vous. L'étonnement de vos spectateurs suivra.

49. LE JOKER

Un de vos jokers possède un singe regardant dans un miroir. Dans ce miroir, vous constaterez qu'on peut y voir une carte. Si vous forcez cette carte, vous pourrez utiliser le joker pour la révéler. Vous trouverez plus bas deux façons simples de forcer une carte. Remettez la carte forcée dans le paquet. Dites alors que vous retrouverez la carte et sortez le joker. Le spectateur dira évidemment que le joker n'est pas sa carte. Demandez ensuite au spectateur d'examiner le miroir de plus près.

50. FORÇAGE EN CROIX !

Avant votre spectacle, placez la carte à forcer sur le dessus du paquet. Demandez à un spectateur de couper la moitié du paquet et le déposer à côté. Prenez la portion du dessous et déposez-la en forme de croix sur la partie coupée. Remémorez aux spectateurs comment le paquet a été mélangé et ensuite coupé, là où le spectateur avait choisi. Soulevez maintenant la partie supérieure et demandez au spectateur de prendre la carte du dessus de la portion inférieure. Cette carte deviendra la carte à forcer.

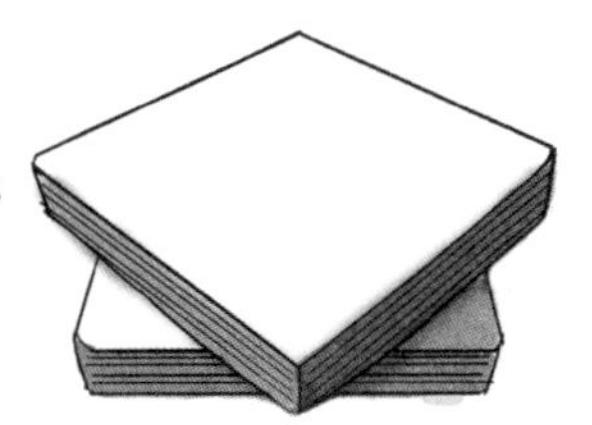

51. LE FORÇAGE 10/20

Positionnez la carte que vous désirez forcer en 9ième position. Demandez à un spectateur de nommer un nombre entre 10 et 20. Demandez-lui ensuite de prendre le paquet et de déposer une carte à la fois sur la table jusqu'au nombre choisi. Demandez-lui d'additionner les 2 chiffres de son nombre (par exemple, si le chiffre choisi est 16 : 1+6=7), et de compter les cartes de cette dernière pile jusqu'au résultat (7, dans ce cas en particulier). Dites ensuite au spectateur que ces cartes sont éliminées, et que la prochaine carte sera la sienne. Bien entendu, cette carte sera la carte que vous cherchez à forcer.

52. LES 21 CARTES !

Distribuez 21 cartes en 3 colonnes de 7, face vers le haut. =Demandez à un spectateur de penser à une carte et de pointer la colonne où elle se trouve. Ramassez les cartes une colonne à la fois sans en changer l'ordre, en vous assurant que la colonne contenant la carte soit entre les deux autres. Recommencer les mêmes étapes, c'est-à-dire distribuez les cartes pour en faire 3 colonnes (en distribuant une carte par colonne en alternance). Demandez encore au spectateur de vous indiquer la colonne où sa carte se trouve. Encore une fois, ramassez les cartes une colonne à la fois sans en changer l'ordre, en vous assurant que la colonne contenant la carte soit entre les deux autres. Répétez les étapes précédentes une troisième fois. Une fois les cartes ramassées dites : « Il me faudra un VRAI MIRACLE pour retrouver votre carte ». Épelez les mots « VRAI MIRACLE » en déposant une carte pour chaque lettre. Retournez la dernière carte au « E » de miracle. C'est la bonne carte !

53. TOUR D'ÉPELLATION

Avant votre spectacle, sortez les cartes de l'as au 10 d'une même couleur et placez-les dans l'ordre suivant à partir du dessus : 3, as, 8, 10, 5, 2, 9, 7, 4 et 6. Dites à vos spectateurs que vous épèlerez les cartes pour les trouver (en ne tenant que ce paquet de 10 cartes). En performance, prenez la carte dessus en disant « A » et remettez-la sous le paquet. Prenez la suivante en disant « S » et retournez-la sur la table en disant que vous avez trouvez l'as. Maintenant prenez la prochaine en disant « D » et mettez-la en dessous. Continuez avec « E » (en-dessous), « U » (en-dessous) et « X » (sur la table; on verra un 2). Continuez avec chaque carte comme ceci et terminez en retournant la dernière et en disant « Dix ».

54. ÉPELLATION EXPERT

Avant votre spectacle, inversez le paquet de 10 cartes de l'effet précédent. Dans ce cas, le 6 serait donc sur le dessus et la carte du dessous serait le 3. Déposez ce paquet de 10 cartes sur le dessus du jeu et demandez à un spectateur de couper le jeu. Comme vous aurez mémorisez la carte-clé (dans ce cas-ci le 6), il vous sera facile de localiser le 6 et de séparer le jeu à cet endroit et le couper à nouveau. Comptez alors les cartes une à une sur la table en comptant dix cartes (vous inverserez ainsi l'ordre et remettrez le paquet dans l'ordre du tour précédent).

55. SUPER TOUR D'ÉPELLATION

Le tour précédent peut être effectué en y ajoutant les cartes de figure. Une fois de plus, nommez une lettre pour chaque carte retournez la carte à la dernière lettre pour démontrer votre prouesse. Ajoutez le valet, la dame et le roi. L'ordre devient donc : 6, As, 8, Roi, 4, 2, 10, 7, Dame, 5, 3, 9 et valet (qui sera la dernière carte).

56. ÉPELLATION SANS AVERTISSEMENT

Utilisons cette fois-ci la carte-clé pour un tour d'épellation différent. Faites choisir et replacer une carte. Prenez le paquet et prétendez chercher la carte. En fait, vous êtes à la recherche de la carte-clé. À partir de cette dernière, repérez la carte choisie et épelez dans votre tête cette carte (en comptant une carte par lettre et ce, à partir de la carte-clé). Si par exemple c'était l'as de trèfle, la carte-clé sera A, la suivante S et ainsi de suite. Coupez le paquet à cet endroit et complétez la coupe. Donnez le paquet à un spectateur et demandez-lui d'épeler le nom de sa carte.

57. ÉPELLATION ET COMPTAGE

Avant votre spectacle, déposez les cartes suivantes dans cet ordre précis (à partir du dessus) : 6 de cœur, 7 de pique, 8 de trèfle, 3 de trèfle, 3 de carreau et 4 de carreau. Ajoutez par-dessus 9 autres cartes. Pendant votre spectacle, dites à un spectateur que vous allez prendre quelques cartes au hasard. Enlevez les 9 cartes du dessus et prenez les six suivantes dans vos mains. Demandez au spectateur de choisir mentalement une de ces cartes. Replacez les 15 cartes (9 + 6) sur le dessus. Donnez le paquet au spectateur et demandez-lui d'épeler sa carte. Peu importe la carte, le tour fonctionnera.

58. LA LETTRE DE GRAND-PÈRE

Sur une feuille de papier, écrivez : « Je savais que tu serais dans le pétrin un jour donc je vais t'aider en te disant que la carte est le 4 de trèfle. Avec Amour, Grand-Papa ». Scellez cette lettre dans une enveloppe et gardez-là dans votre poche. Pendant votre spectacle, forcez le 4 de trèfle (tel que décris plus tôt). Demandez au spectateur de remettre sa carte et de mélanger le jeu. Prétendez être incapable de retrouver la carte. Dites finalement : « Il n'y qu'une solution. Il y a un an, mon grand-père m'a envoyé une lettre me disant qu'elle pouvait m'aider dans les moments les plus sombres ». Sortez la lettre et donnez-la au spectateur pour qu'il puisse la lire. Terminez en disant : « Ah ce Grand-Papa, lui, il l'a ».

59. LA LETTRE PROFESSIONNELLE

Pour un impact encore plus frappant, pourquoi ne pas vous adressez la lettre et l'envoyer par la poste ? De cette façon, le timbre et le cachet de la poste augmenterait l'authenticité de l'effet. Profitez-en pour froissez un peu l'enveloppe pour lui donner un air encore plus vrai !

60. RENVERSEMENT INVISIBLE

Pour ce tour, vous aurez besoin de votre paquet Dextérité et d'un paquet normal. Insérez le 5 de cœur (5C) face vers le haut dans votre paquet normal. Remettez le paquet dans sa boite. Utilisez votre paquet Dextérité pour forcer le 5C en disant : « Je vais tenter de retourner une carte dans l'autre paquet ». Prétendez sortir une carte invisible du paquet régulier, la retourner et la replacer. Sortez le paquet de sa boite et montrez la carte renversée. Demandez le nom de la carte et prouvez que vous aviez vu juste.

61. FACTEUR 'X'

Sur le dos du 10 de carreau de votre paquet normal, inscrivez un gros « X » avec un marqueur. Insérez cette carte environ au centre du paquet. Forcez le 10 de carreau en affirmant : « Voici le trésor légendaire marqué d'un gros « X ». Demandez au spectateur de prendre l'autre paquet pour voir s'il contient quelque chose de spécial. Le spectateur trouvera évidemment la carte avec le « X ». Incroyable !

62. DISPARUE

Enlevez la carte que vous désirez forcer de votre paquet régulier et déposez-la dans votre poche. Forcez cette carte et demandez au spectateur de prendre l'autre paquet et d'aller chercher sa carte. Évidemment il ne la trouvera pas puisqu'elle n'est plus là. Sortez-la de votre poche et montrez que vous aviez prédit la carte qu'il choisirait.

63. LA CARTE À L'ORANGE

Vous pourriez mettre votre carte supplémentaire dans une foule d'objets, comme par exemple dans votre portefeuille, un ballon, une bouteille ou une orange. La disparition de la carte du paquet ordinaire accentue l'effet. Si par exemple vous utilisez une orange, forcez une carte du paquet Dextérité et demandez au spectateur quelle est la carte choisie. Dites que vous allez faire disparaitre

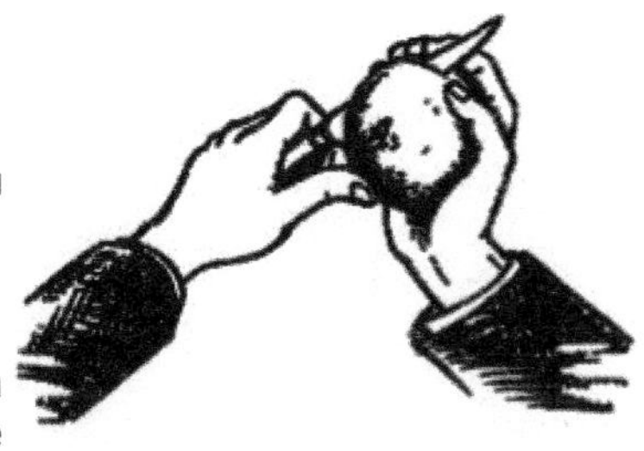

la carte de l'autre jeu et la faire réapparaitre dans l'orange. Le public croira que c'est une blague et tous seront surpris de constater votre prouesse.
Pour préparer l'illusion, faites un trou dans une orange avec un crayon. Le crayon ne doit pas transpercer l'orange au complet. Façonnez un tube avec la carte à forcer, et insérez la dans le trou de l'orange. Après avoir forcé la carte, coupez le fruit en deux et révélez la carte choisie. Pour les plus jeunes, assurez-vous d'avoir l'aide d'un adulte.

64. LA CARTE À L'ORANGE EXTREME

Pour avoir l'air d'un vrai pro, enlevez le pédoncule de l'orange, faites votre trou et déposez la carte. Replacez le pédoncule et collez-le avec de la colle caoutchouc. Vous pouvez maintenant montrer l'orange sous chaque angle avant de révéler la carte. Les détails comme celui-ci qui font toute la différence entre un tour de magie correct et une présentation professionnelle !

65. LE CHOIX DU MAGICIEN

Dans un bol, déposez une orange (préparée) ainsi qu'une banane et une pomme. Demandez à un spectateur de choir un des 3 fruits. S'il choisit l'orange, référez-vous au tour précédent. S'il choisit la pomme ou la banane, mettez ce fruit de côté et dites : « Parfait, nous éliminons ce fruit ». Demandez encore une fois de choisir un des deux autres fruits. S'il choisit cette fois l'orange, faites comme au tour précédent. S'il choisit l'autre fruit, prenez-le en disant : « excellent, nous avons maintenant éliminé deux fruits, il ne reste que l'orange ». Cette technique se nomme LE CHOIX DU MAGICIEN. C'est une technique idéale pour forcer l'objet de votre choix.

66. EMBOUTEILLÉ

Ouvrez une bouteille de boisson gazeuse et buvez-en un peu. Roulez la carte à forcer et insérez-là dans la bouteille. Aidez-vous de la gomme d'un crayon pour redresser la carte le mieux possible. Ce travail minutieux en vaut la peine ! Une fois le travail accompli, remettez le bouchon. Après avoir fait disparaitre la carte forcée, faites déboucher la bouteille par un spectateur. Versez le contenu dans un verre et attirez l'attention sur la carte à l'intérieur. Les gens se creuseront les méninges.

67. SOUS LA BOUTEILLE !

Avant votre spectacle, écrivez, sous une bouteille de boisson gazeuse, « 10 de cœur ». Pendant votre spectacle, déposez une carte quelconque sous la bouteille en disant que vous y reviendrez sous peu. Forcez le 10 de cœur et remettez-le dans le paquet. Dites : « ne serait-ce pas incroyable si votre carte se trouvait sous la bouteille ? » Le spectateur lève alors la bouteille pour trouver la mauvaise carte. Dites alors : « Non, je voulais vraiment dire sous la bouteille, regardez en dessous ! » Il tournera la bouteille et verra les mots « 10 de cœur ».

68. VOUS NE L'OUBLIEREZ PAS

Voici une bonne blague à faire entre vos miracles. Forcez une carte, demandez au spectateur de la mémoriser et de la remettre dans le paquet. En mélangeant le paquet, dites : « vous ne l'oublierez pas n'est-ce pas ? » Pour vous aider, répétez « 3 de trèfle, 3 de trèfle ». Évidemment, vous ne faites que dire la carte forcée. Vos spectateurs seront surpris et se mettront à rire !

69. L'ART DE LA MANIPULATION DES CARTES

Votre paquet marqué peut aussi être utilisé comme un paquet normal. Il vous est possible de faire plusieurs tours et manipulations comme avec un paquet normal. Vous trouverez ici quelques tours et manipulations qui ne nécessitent pas l'utilisation du système de marquage. En fait vous pouvez utiliser n'importe quel paquet. Pourquoi ne pas l'emprunter ?

70. LA CASCADE

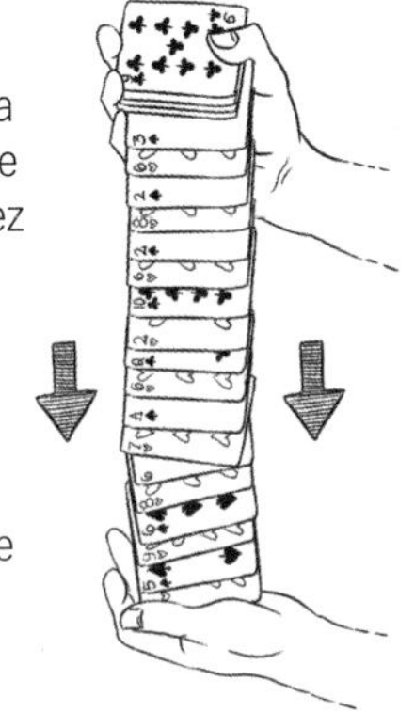

L'objectif ici est de laisser tomber les cartes de la main droite vers la main gauche dans un mouvement continuel. Ça vous demandera de la pratique mais c'est plus facile que vous ne le pensez. Commencez d'abord avec la moitié du jeu. Tenez le paquet par les extrémités entre vos doigts et votre pouce. Courbez le jeu légèrement vers votre paume en exerçant une pression. Tenez votre main gauche sous la droite, environ 10 centimètres plus bas. Relâchez légèrement la pression. Les cartes se libéreront une à une de votre main droite pour tomber dans votre main gauche. Augmentez la distance jusqu'à 30 cm.

71. LA VOLÉE DES CARTES

Ceci est similaire à la cascade de cartes mais au lieu d'utiliser une légère pression, vous en exercerez une plus grande pour que les cartes puissent vraiment sortir de votre main droite rapidement vers votre main gauche. Comme vous l'avez fait dans la cascade, prenez la moitié du paquet et courbez-le vers l'intérieur. Augmentez la pression et les cartes voleront de votre main droite vers la gauche. Commencez avec vos mains assez proches l'une de l'autre et augmentez graduellement la distance.

72. LA COUPE À UNE MAIN

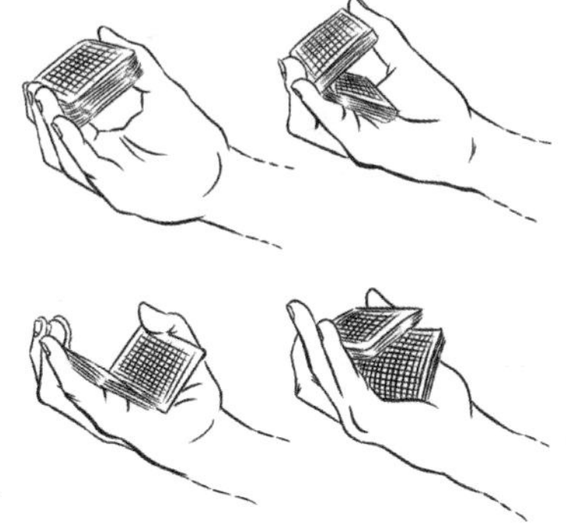

Couper un paquet n'est pas impressionnant en soi, mais avec cette technique, nommée « la coupe Charlier », vous pourrez l'effectuer avec une seule main. Commencez en tenant le paquet au-dessus de votre paume droite en utilisant seulement le bout de 4 doigts. Votre pouce va maintenant relâcher la pression sur la moitié inférieure du paquet ce qui fera tomber la moitié des cartes dans votre paume. Utilisez votre index pour pousser ce paquet vers le haut et contre votre pouce (en forme de tente). Relâchez maintenant la partie supérieure sur votre paume tout en poussant sur la partie inférieure avec votre pouce. Repositionnez le paquet. Vous venez d'effectuer une coupe à une seule main.

73. L'ÉTALEMENT DES CARTES

Note : Éviter d'utiliser cette technique sur une table lisse car les cartes glisseront. Agrippez le paquet avec le pouce d'un côté et le majeur de l'autre. Votre index doit être sur le dessus. Sur une nappe ou sur un tapis de poker, étalez les cartes rapidement et d'un seul mouvement tout en poussant sur le dessus du paquet avec votre index. Pratiquez jusqu'à ce que les cartes forment une ligne droite. Retournez la carte qui se trouve sous le paquet et appuyez légèrement dessus. Toutes les autres cartes se retourneront également face vers le haut.

74. COMMENT LANCER UNE CARTE

Voici une technique qui vous permettra de lancer des cartes somme dans le film Insaisissable 2. Pour de plus amples détails, référez-vous aux liens vidéo inclus dans ce manuel. Prenez une carte et tenez-la légèrement entre le pouce et l'index. Courbez les doigts et la main vers vous. Finalement, lancez rapidement la carte tout en dépliant vos doigts (un peu comme un frisbee). Bravo, vous venez d'apprendre comment lancer une carte. Avec un peu de pratique, vous réussirez à transpercer du styromousse ou même un fruit.

75. VOUS N'AVEZ PLUS DE CARTES

Pour ce tour, vous devrez fabriquer une carte spéciale. Avec un marqueur, écrivez sur une carte : « Vous n'avez plus de carte ». Utilisez un marqueur qui sera très visible et une carte où il y a beaucoup d'espace blanc (comme un 2 de cœur). Placez cette carte en 21ième position. Demandez à un spectateur de couper un petit paquet. Il doit prendre moins de 21 cartes donc guidez-le sinon l'effet sera trop long. Demandez au spectateur de tenir ces cartes dans son dos pour ne pas que vous puissiez voir le nombre de cartes. Commencez à compter 21 cartes sur la table en comptant dans votre tête et en disant que vous avez besoin de quelques cartes. Prenez cette pile, retournez la carte du dessus pour ensuite la déposer sur la table. Demandez ensuite au spectateur de retourner une de ses cartes et de la déposer sur la vôtre. Continuez de la sorte jusqu'à ce que le spectateur ait retourné toutes ses cartes. Immédiatement après celle-ci, vous retournerez la prochaine carte, qui est celle où vous aviez inscrit le message ci-dessus. Si vous suivez les étapes à la lettre, l'effet fonctionnera parfaitement et les spectateurs n'y verront que du feu.

76. LES CARTES TÉLÉPATHIQUES

Le magicien montre 3 cartes et demande à un spectateur de penser à l'une d'elle. Le magicien dépose ensuite les cartes dans sa poche. Il en sort finalement deux et les déposent sur la table. Si vous avez pensé à votre carte, c'est celle qui est restée dans ma poche. Quelle est votre carte? « Le 3 de trèfle » répond le spectateur. Le magicien sort la carte de la poche : le 3 de trèfle. La solution est simple : vous devez avoir deux autres cartes dans votre poche. En mettant les trois cartes dans votre poche, mémorisez leur ordre. Sortez les deux autres cartes et déposez-les sur la table. Les spectateurs croiront que ce sont les deux cartes du début. Quand le spectateur nomme sa carte, vous n'avez qu'à ressortir la bonne carte. Voilà !

77. LA CARTE MONTANTE

Voici comment faire monter une carte du milieu du jeu comme par magie. Sortez trois cartes du paquet. Enfilez un élastique autour du paquet (sur la longueur). Divisez maintenant le paquet en deux en séparant les 2 bouts (voir photo 2). Déposez une des trois cartes sur l'une des deux moitiés (et sur l'élastique). Refermez les 2 moitiés ensemble (en tenant le tout fermement sinon l'élastique fera sortir cette carte). Déposez les 2 autres cartes, l'une dessus et l'autre dessous le paquet pour bien dissimuler l'élastique. Maintenant l'ensemble a l'aspect d'un paquet normal. Utilisez une pince pour maintenir l'ensemble en place. Pendant votre spectacle, enlevez la pince en tenant le paquet fermement. En montrant le paquet aux spectateurs, relâchez la pression sur le jeu. La carte montera tout doucement, créant un effet quelque peu effarant.

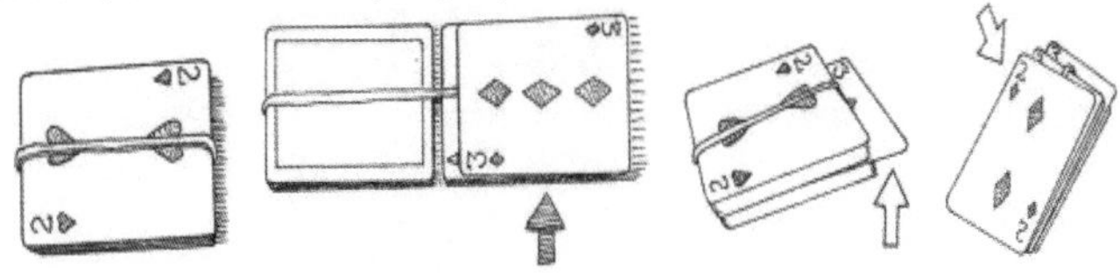

78. LA MONTÉE DES AS !

Reproduises les étapes du tour précédent, mais cette fois en insérant les quatre as au centre du paquet. Affirmez à la foule devoir trouver les as. Relâchez subitement la pression, pour faire sortir les as du paquet.

79. LA CARTE CHOISIE ET MONTANTE

Commencez par couper (en vous faisant aider) une longue incision sur le dos d'une boite de cartes. L'incision doit être de la longueur du design sur la boite (ne pas couper jusqu'aux ailerons) et environ 1 cm de largeur. Lorsque vous insérez le paquet dans la boite, assurez-vous que le design soit vers le haut, camouflant l'incision. Gardez néanmoins ce côté vers le bas sur la table. Lorsque vous êtes prêt, sortez le paquet en redéposant la boite sut la table avec l'incision vers le bas. Faites choisir une carte et remettez-la sur le dessus du paquet. Remettez le paquet dans la boite (toujours avec le design face à l'incision). Gardez la boite ouverte et tenez-la entre votre pouce d'un côté et vos doigts du côté de l'incision. Avec votre index, faites glisser la carte du dessus vers l'ouverture de la boite. La carte semble sortir par elle-même.

80. LE REGARD SECRET

Expliquez au public que vous avez des yeux au bout des doigts. Pour le prouver, vous prenez le paquet et commencez à déposer les cartes une à une sur la table. Demandez au public vous arrêter à leur gré. Lorsqu'ils vous indiquent d'arrêter, prenez la prochaine carte et montrez-la au public sans que vous puissiez la voir. Agrippez la carte en haut et en bas avec votre main droite. Avec votre index gauche, exercez une légère pression au centre de la carte. Cette pression fera courber la carte légèrement, vous permettant de constater l'index de cette carte. Nommez simplement la carte, prouvant aux spectateurs que vous avez des yeux au bout des doigts.

81. LES ROIS ONT UNE DOUBLURE

Sortez les valets et les rois d'un paquet et prenez les quatre valets dans votre main droite. Déposez un roi par-dessus les valets, et ensuite les trois autres, mais en leur donnant la forme d'un éventail. Pour le public, vous semblez ne tenir que quatre rois. Une fois les quatre rois montrés, déposez-les face vers le bas sur le dessus du jeu. Prenez les cartes (une à une) sur le dessus du jeu (les valets) et insérez-les à différents endroits dans le paquet. Gardez bien entendu les cartes face vers le bas. Claquez des doigts et retournez les 4 cartes du dessus (les rois). Vous pouvez faire un éventail avec le paquet pour monter qu'il n'y a pas d'autres rois.

82. LES ROIS ONT UNE DOUBLURE 2

Pour les débutants, voici une version simplifiée du tour précédent. Retirez les 4 rois d'un autre paquet identique. Déposez les 8 rois sur le dessus du jeu. Durant votre spectacle, prenez les 4 premières cartes et faites-en un éventail pour les montrer clairement au public. Insérez-les un à un à différents endroits du paquet. Claquez des doigts et prenez les rois du dessus du paquet pour montrer qu'ils sont revenus sur le dessus. Déposez-les ensuite dans votre poche. Claquez encore des doigts et faites un éventail du paquet sur la table en montrant que les rois sont revenus dans le jeu..

83. LE SYSTÈME POINTEUR

En regardant votre paquet, vous vous rendrez compte que certaines cartes sont des « pointeurs ». Par exemple, regardez le 7 de pique. Il y a sept piques sur la carte, dont 5 qui pointent dans la même direction. Les as sont des pointeurs ainsi que les 3, 5, 6, 8 et 9. Prenez toutes les cartes « pointeurs » et orientez-les dans la même direction pour ensuite déposer ce paquet de pointeurs dans le centre du jeu. Faites choisir une carte en étalant les cartes face vers le bas de façon à ce qu'une de ces cartes soit choisie. Alors que le spectateur montre sa carte, tournez le paquet (en le gardant face vers le bas). Demandez au spectateur de remettre sa carte au centre. Étalez les cartes avec les faces vers vous (et les dos face aux spectateurs). Il sera facile pour vous de trouver la bonne carte car elle sera la seule pointant dans la direction opposée.

84. LA LIGNE EST MINCE

Pour ce tour, dessinez une ligne mince sur le côté du jeu. Pendant votre spectacle, faites choisir une carte. Alors que le spectateur regarde sa carte, tournez le paquet. Demandez au spectateur de remettre la carte où il le désire. Pour retrouver sa carte, vous n'avez qu'à trouver la marque de crayon qui se trouve de l'autre côté de la ligne.

85. SORTEZ-MOI DE LÀ !

Une autre façon de retrouver une carte est d'assembler toutes les cartes d'une même couleur (par exemple les cœurs) pour les insérer ensemble au centre du paquet. Faites choisir une carte en vous assurant que le spectateur évite les cartes du centre. Faites replacer cette carte au centre. Il vous sera évidemment facile de retrouver la carte puisqu'elle sera la seule qui n'est pas en cœur.

86. LE COIN PLIÉ

Dans ce tour, le magicien fait un éventail de cartes avec les faces vers les spectateurs pour ensuite demander à quelqu'un de toucher une des cartes. Dès qu'un spectateur touche la carte, le magicien, de son pouce gauche caché derrière le paquet, plie légèrement un coin. Même si vous mélangez ensuite le paquet, vous pourrez facilement repérer la carte comportant le pli dans un des coins.

87. RAYON X
Le magicien sort un paquet de carte de la boite et tient cette boite dans son dos. Il demande à quelqu'un de choisir une carte du jeu et de l'insérer dans la boite. La boite est ensuite refermée. Le magicien, malgré l'impossibilité de voir la carte, porte la boite à son front et est instantanément capable de nommer la carte et ce même si personne ne l'a vue. Avant votre spectacle, coupez un petit trou dans le coin inférieur droit de la boite. Gardez votre pouce sur le trou pour le dissimuler. Lorsque vous portez la boite à votre front, retirez votre pouce, vous montrant rapidement la carte choisie.

88. LE PAQUET QUI CHANGE DE COULEUR
Séparez les cartes rouges des cartes noires et arrangez les deux portions avec soin de la façon suivante: insérez une section dans l'autre mais ne poussez pas les deux parties au complet. Les cartes seront maintenant en alternance, une noire, une rouge etc. Positionnez un joker en dessous du paquet. En effeuillant les cartes d'un côté, seules les cartes rouges seront visibles. En changeant de main, tournez le paquet bout pour bout. Cette fois-ci, en effeuillant, seules les cartes noires seront visibles. Pour terminer, poussez les 2 sections complètement l'une dans l'autre. La troisième fois que vous effeuillerez le paquet, il sera normal et peut même être vérifié par un spectateur.

89. PAIRS ET IMPAIRS
Un paquet est divisé en deux parties. Un spectateur choisit une carte d'une des parties et la remet dans l'autre. Cette partie du paquet doit maintenant être mélangée. Le magicien peut malgré tout, retrouver très aisément la carte. Dans la première moitié, il n'y a que les cartes impaires (as, 3,5,7, 9, valets et rois) alors que dans l'autre on ne retrouve que les cartes paires. Personne ne constatera ce subterfuge. Lorsqu'une carte est choisie dans une section et replacée dans l'autre, il vous est donc très facile de la repérer.

90. LA PAIRE DES IMPAIRS
Le magicien et un spectateur prennent chacun un petit paquet de cartes. Le magicien dit ensuite : « Comptez vos cartes. Lorsque nous y additionnerons le nombre de cartes en ma possession, la somme sera paire si vous avez un nombre impair de cartes, et impaire si vous un nombre pair de cartes ». Pour réussir cet effet, vous n'avez qu'à prendre un nombre impair de cartes, ce qui assure le succès du tour.

91. JUSTE UNE BLAGUE
Il est toujours intéressant d'avoir quelques blagues dans votre répertoire entre vos miracles. Faites choisir trois cartes et remettez-les dans le paquet. Dites : « voulez-vous que je les retrouve en même temps ou une à la fois ? » Si on vous répond « en même temps », lancez le paquet dans les airs. Si on vous répond « une à la fois », lancez les cartes une à une. Peu importe la réponse, c'est une blague qui fera certainement rire tous et chacun.

92. UNE AUTRE BONNE BLAGUE
Faites choisir une carte et demandez au spectateur de penser à la valeur de sa carte et d'y ajouter trois. Demandez-lui ensuite de multiplier cette somme par deux, d'additionner cinq, de soustraire sept, etc. (vous pouvez continuer longtemps comme ça). Après avoir fait durer le plaisir, demandez au spectateur de vous révéler son nombre. Soyez pensif et révélez n'importe quelle carte. Vous aurez tort mais les gens auront bien ri.

93. SÉRIEUSEMENT BONNE

De temps à autre, en effectuant le tour précédent, vous révélerez par hasard la carte choisie, ce qui en fera un miracle. Les magiciens les plus futés réaliseront rapidement qu'il est possible de forcer la carte de façon à toujours retrouver celle-ci à la fin de l'effet.

MAGIE AVEC OBJETS DE TOUS LES JOURS

94. UN POUCE CASSÉ

Dans ce tour classique, vous semblez casser votre pouce pour ensuite lui redonner une apparence normale, sans aucune blessure. Votre main gauche doit être paumée vers vous avec le pouce pointant vers le haut. Pliez le pouce gauche de façon à ce qu'il pointe vers vous. Pliez également votre pouce droit et positionnez-le à côté du pouce gauche (votre index droit cache l'écart entre les 2 pouces). Pratiquez ceci pour que la préparation soit à l'insu de tous. Du point de vue des spectateurs, ils verront que vous avez mis votre index par-dessus votre pouce gauche. Bougez votre main droite vers la droite. Voilà, votre pouce est séparé de sa main. Bougez votre main droite vers la gauche pour replacer votre pouce. Laissez vos mains tomber rapidement de chaque côté et dites : « N'essayez pas ceci à la maison, à moins d'être magicien ! »

95. J'AI CASSÉ MON DOIGT

Accessoire requis : vos doigts !

1. Pourquoi ne s'en tenir qu'au pouce ? Ce tour est un peu plus difficile à maîtriser, mais il en vaut la peine, car l'illusion est parfaite.
Joignez vos 2 mains et mettez votre index droit sous les doigts de la main gauche alors que le majeur, l'annulaire et l'auriculaire vont par-dessus.
2. Sous votre main gauche, votre pouce droit pousse l'index droit en le pliant vers la droite.
3. Deux choses se passent simultanément quand les deux mains se séparent (avec un SNAP !). Premièrement, pliez votre index gauche vers l'intérieur et ensuite, le majeur, l'annulaire et l'auriculaire de la main droite se plient un peu pour exposer l'index droit.
L'illusion est si parfaite que les gens peuvent même s'exclamer !
Rassemblez vos mains à nouveau et relaxez un moment. Terminez en disant : « Une chance que je suis un magicien sinon, j'aurais peut-être un peu de douleur ! ».

96. LE DOIGT QUI ALLONGE !

Accessoire requis : vos doigts !

La magie effectuée avec les doigts est impressionnante. En voici un autre exemple. Vous donnerez ici l'illusion que votre doigt allonge. Pour débuter, placez-vous comme si vous alliez vous « casser » le doigt. Au lieu de séparer les mains, faites comme sur l'illustration avec l'index gauche au-dessus de l'index droit (le bout de l'index gauche caché plié sous l'index droit). Lorsque vous êtes en position, montrez que votre index est très long. L'angle est critique dans ce tour alors...pratiquez devant un miroir !

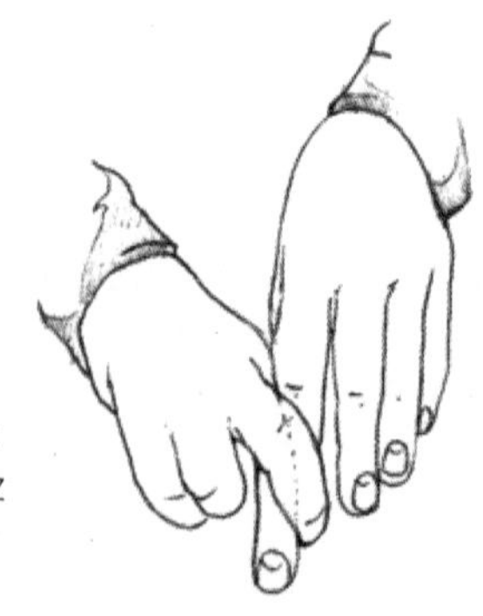

97. L'APPARITION D'UN HOT DOG !

Accessoire requis : les doigts d'un spectateur !

Cet effet n'est pas tant un tour de magie qu'une illusion d'optique. Affirmez à un spectateur que vous ferez apparaître un hot dog dans les airs et qu'il sera le seul à le voir. Dites au spectateur de tenir ses deux index collés par le bout des doigts et de les séparer tranquillement tout en relaxant ses yeux. Il doit faire ceci proche de ses yeux. Essayez-le vous-même, vous verrez un petit hot dog apparaître entre vos deux doigts. L'illusion est due au croisement de votre vision. Chaque bout du hot dog est en réalité le bout de vos doigts.

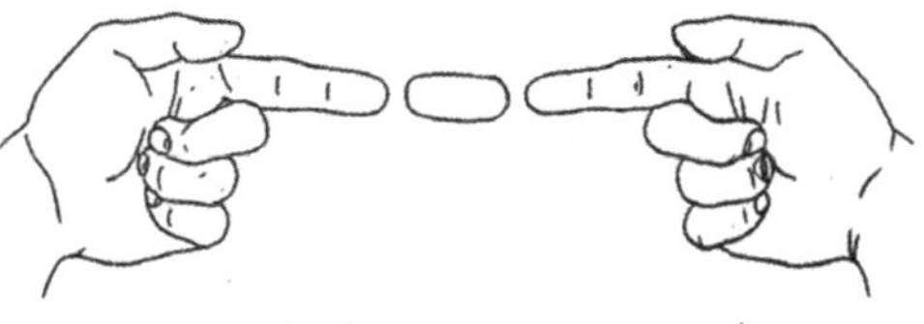

98. LES TROMBONES ENCHAÎNÉS

Accessoires requis : deux trombones et un billet de banque.

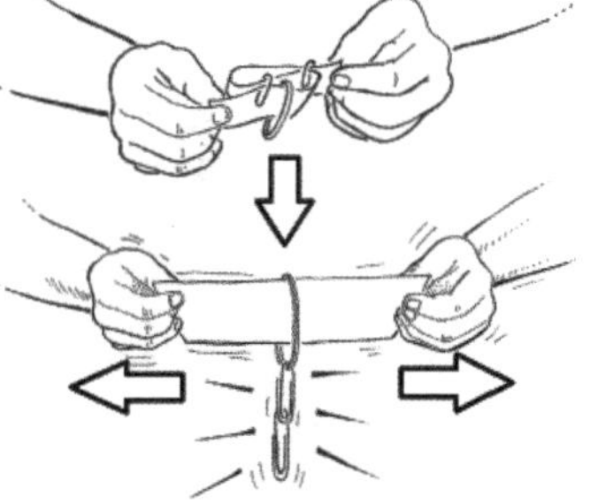

Pour cet effet, vous devrez vous munir de deux trombones et d'un billet de cinq dollars. Vous pourriez également utiliser un bout de papier. Avec le billet de cinq dollars, formez un « S » et disposez les trombones comme sur l'illustration. Si vous tirez sur les deux bouts, les deux trombones voleront dans les airs et s'enchaîneront d'eux-mêmes !

99. UPER ENCHAÎNEMENT

Accessoires requis : deux trombones, un billet de banque et un élastique

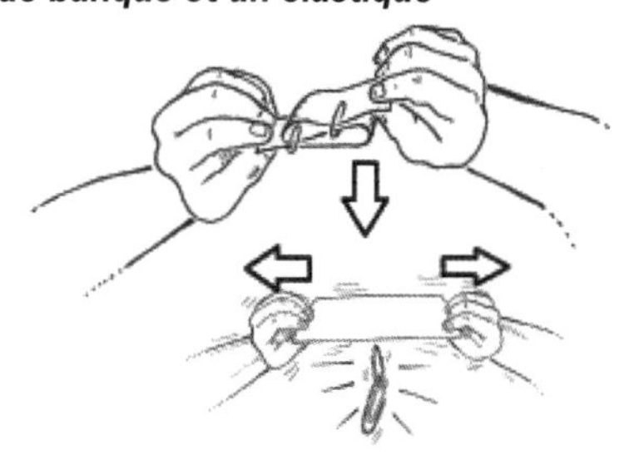

Si vous ajoutez un élastique comme sur la photo, l'illusion sera encore plus impressionnante. Faites exactement comme sur la photo et, prenez une grande respiration en tirant sur les bouts du billet. Les deux trombones s'enchaîneront et l'un des deux s'enchaînera sur l'élastique. Ce tour est utilisé par plusieurs magiciens professionnels.

100. L'ÉLASTIQUE QUI SAUTE

Accessoire requis : un élastique

Vous aurez bien sûr besoin d'un élastique. Disposez un élastique autour de votre index et votre majeur et refermez la main avec les doigts pointant vers vous. En fermant votre main, assurez-vous que tous vos doigts sont à l'intérieur de l'élastique (seulement le bout des doigts). Aidez-vous de votre autre main. Du point de vue du public, l'impression est que seuls deux de vos doigts sont à l'intérieur. Dites quelques mots magiques et ouvrez vos doigts. L'élastique changera automatiquement de place sur l'annulaire et l'auriculaire.

101. L'ÉLASTIQUE EXTRÊME QUI SAUTE !

Accessoires requis : deux élastiques

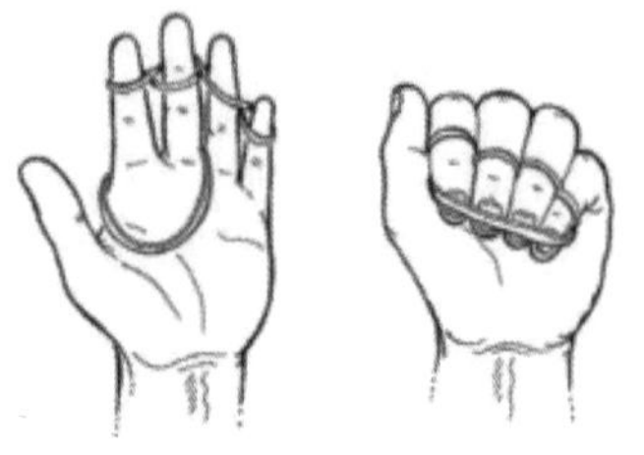

Si vous tournez un deuxième élastique autour de vos doigts comme illustré, il sera encore plus difficile d'exécuter ce tour (en réalité, il n'y a aucun changement mais les spectateurs ne le savent pas). Vous donnerez l'illusion que l'élastique ne peut pas s'évader, mais si vous performez le tour tel que décrit, tout est possible. Ce tour est idéal immédiatement après le tour précédent.

102. DOUBLE SAUT

Accessoires requis : deux élastiques

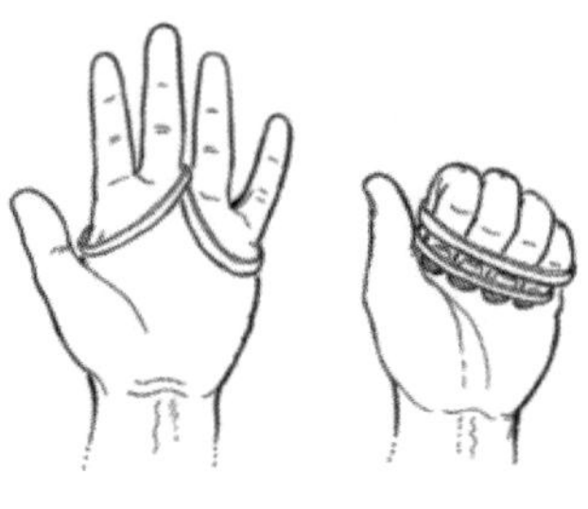

Une suite logique fait appel à deux élastiques de couleurs différentes. Mettez l'un des deux sur vos deux premiers doigts alors que l'autre va sur les deux autres. Fermez la main avec les doigts qui pointent vers vous. Chaque doigt doit entrer dans un des deux élastiques. Encore une fois, aidez-vous de votre autre main. Quand vous ouvrez la main, les deux élastiques changeront de place. Ce tour fonctionnera même avec un troisième élastique au bout des doigts. Quel effet !

103. FRISSONS AU RENDEZ-VOUS !

Accessoires requis : un élastique brisé et une bague

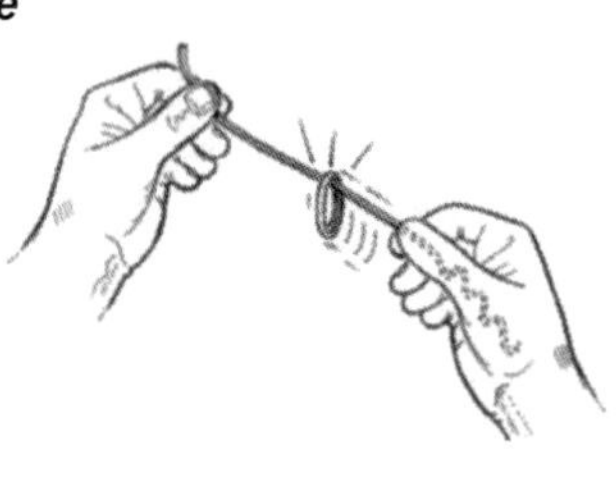

Si vous avez un brisé un de vos élastiques, vous pouvez quand même l'utiliser pour un tour. Empruntez une bague et passez-y l'élastique. Maintenez l'élastique dans le centre avec une main (cachez également le reste de l'élastique dans cette même main). De l'autre main, tenez l'autre bout et étirez-le pour que l'élastique vers le haut. Très lentement, relâchez légèrement la tension de l'élastique, libérant du coup la partie cachée de celui-ci. La bague bougera alors d'elle-même vers le haut. L'illusion ne sera que meilleure si vous ralentissez votre geste au maximum.

104. LE BALLON INCREVABLE

Accessoires nécessaires : un ballon de fête, du ruban adhésif transparent et une punaise

Gonflez un ballon de fête et collez plusieurs bouts de ruban adhésif à différents endroits. Pendant votre spectacle, prenez des aiguilles et entrez-les dans le ballon où il y a du ruban adhésif. Grâce au ruban, le ballon n'éclatera pas !

105. LE CRAYON DISPARAIT !

Accessoires requis : un crayon et un foulard

Tenez un crayon ou un stylo dans la main gauche. Demandez à un membre de l'auditoire de draper un mouchoir sur le crayon. Au même moment étendez votre index gauche et laissez le crayon glisser dans votre manche. Comptez jusqu'à trois et demandez à votre assistant de fouetter le mouchoir au loin. Au compte de trois, placez votre index vers le bas les spectateurs croiront que le crayon a disparu !

106. LA ROCHE ROULANTE !

Accessoires requis : un long fil noir, une bague et une petite roche ou une bille

Prenez un long bout de fil à coudre noir et attachez-le à une bague. Placez la bague au centre de la table et déposez le fil de façon à ce qu'il descende de la table là où vous serez assis. Couvrez le tout avec une nappe. Affirmez qu'il vous est possible de contrôler mentalement une roche en la faisant bouger sur la table. Déposez une petite roche directement sur la bague. Prétendez faire d'intenses efforts de concentration et tirez sur le fil secret. La roche semble bouger d'elle-même.

107. L'ŒUF EN ÉQUILIBRE

Accessoires nécessaires : Un œuf et la même préparation avec fil/bague comme expliqué précédemment.

Déposez l'œuf en équilibre sur la bague (qui est toujours cachée sous la nappe). Quand vous retirez l'œuf, tirez le fil pour enlever la bague.

108. L'APPARITION DE LA BALLE

Accessoires requis : Un œuf et la même préparation fil/bague du tour précédent.

Le magicien montre ses mains vides. Il prétend attraper un objet dans les airs et fait apparaître une balle. Prenez un bout de fil de 8 cm (3 pouces) et attachez-le à une bague. Collez l'autre bout à une balle. Quand la bague est portée à votre annulaire et que vos doigts pointent vers le haut, la balle est hors de vue derrière votre main. Lorsque vous secouez votre main vers le haut et légèrement vers l'avant, la balle ira directement au bout de vos doigts.

109. LA BALLE VOLANTE

Accessoires requis : une balle de ping-pong (tennis de table) ainsi qu'un long bout de fil noir (ou fil de pêche) attaché en boucle.

Une balle est tenue dans une main. L'instant suivant, la balle glisse lentement et magiquement dans l'autre main. Le secret de cet effet réside dans la boucle de fil noir. Cette dernière est sur la table avec la balle de ping-pong déposée par-dessus. Alors que vous prenez la balle, faites entrer vos pouces dans la boucle. Levez vos mains avec la boucle entre celles-ci. La balle semblera flotter. Avec de la pratique, vous pourrez faire « flotter » la balle d'une main à l'autre.

110. LES BALLES DE GOLF EN ÉQUILIBRE

Accessoires requis : deux balles de golf et un petit bout de cire.

Mettre en équilibre deux balles de golf l'une par-dessus l'autre semble impossible. Et ce le serait si ce n'était de ce tour. Une petite quantité de cire déposée sur une des deux balles est tout ce que vous nécessitez pour réussir ce tour. La deuxième balle est appuyée contre celle du dessous de façon à faire coller les deux balles ensemble. La balle du dessus semble être en équilibre parfait. Vous pouvez évidemment enlever secrètement la cire et donner les balles à vos amis pour qu'ils essaient le même tour.

111. LES VERRES ANTI-GRAVITÉ

Accessoires requis : deux verres de papier, une agrafe, un livre, un journal et votre baguette magique.

Collez l'agrafe sur un livre avec du ruban, en disposant les pointes de l'agrafe vers le haut (prenez soin de ne pas vous blesser). Couvrez le livre d'un papier journal pour dissimuler l'agrafe. Quand vous êtes prêt, prenez les deux verres de papier et appuyez sur l'agrafe (les pointes transperceront la feuille de papier journal). Assurez-vous d'avoir un verre différent au-dessus de chaque pointe. Disposez maintenant votre baguette magique entre les verres. Levez le tout et tournez le livre tout en gardant la baguette entre les verres. La pression exercée par la baguette sur les verres et l'agrafe donnera l'illusion que les verres sont suspendus.

112. UN AUTRE VERRE ANTI-GRAVITÉ !

Accessoires requis : un verre de papier et une boucle de ruban adhésif (ou un bout de ruban adhésif double face)

Pour débuter, faites une boucle avec le ruban (côté collant vers l'extérieur) et portez cette boucle sur votre pouce comme si c'était une bague. Pendant votre spectacle, prenez le verre et appuyez doucement mais fermement votre pouce contre celui-ci. Lâchez maintenant la prise sur le verre. Le verre semble flotter grâce au ruban adhésif. Vous pouvez aussi utiliser un bout de ruban adhésif double face en collant un côté sur votre pouce.

113. ET UN DERNIER VERRE ANTI-GRAVITÉ

Accessoire requis : Un verre de styromousse

Pendant votre spectacle, montrez un verre de styromousse vide à votre auditoire. Indiquez au public que le ferez flotter. En prenant le verre, appuyez-y votre pouce jusqu'à ce que vous perciez un petit trou (effectuez cette manœuvre lentement pour ne pas qu'on puisse entendre le verre se perforer). N'insérez que le bout de votre pouce dans le verre et relâchez ensuite le verre. Il semblera flotter. Refermez la main sur le verre et sortez votre doigt. Vous pouvez alors cacher le trou avec votre pouce.

114. LA BOUTEILLE ANTI-GRAVITÉ

Accessoire requis : une petite bouteille de cola au moins à moitié pleine.

Ce tour est vraiment rusé car la bouteille peut être examinée à la fin. Empruntez une bouteille de cola d'un spectateur. Affirmez que vous la ferez flotter. Dévisser un peu le bouchon pour faire sortir un peu d'air. Juste sous l'étiquette, appuyez fermement avec votre pouce pour libérer un petit espace vous permettant d'insérer votre pouce entre l'étiquette et la bouteille. Relâchez la bouteille et celle-ci semblera flotter dans les airs. Refermez la main autour de la bouteille. Tout en revissant le bouchon, comprimez légèrement la bouteille pour effacer toute trace. Redonnez la bouteille au spectateur. Personne ne saura comment vous avez réussi!

115. LE HOCHET

Accessoires requis : 4 boites d'allumettes vides, des pièces de monnaie ou des boutons et un élastique

Avant votre spectacle, déposez des pièces de monnaie ou des boutons dans une des boites d'allumettes. Attachez cette boite à votre poignet droit au moyen d'un élastique et recouvrez de votre manche pour bien cacher la boite. Pendant votre spectacle, montrez les 3 boites d'allumettes. Si vous agitez les deux premières boites avec votre main gauche, il n'y aura aucun son. Mais si vous agitez la troisième boite avec votre main droite, on entendra le son des pièces dans la boite cachée. Mélangez maintenant les boites et demandez à un spectateur de deviner laquelle est la boite pleine. Peu importe sa réponse, secouez la boite de votre main gauche pour montrer que la boite est vide. Prenez une des deux autres boites de votre main droite et secouez-la et dites : « non, c'est celle-ci ». Vous pouvez recommencer ce stratagème autant de fois que vous le voulez.

116. LE JOURNAL COUPÉ EST RECONSTITUÉ

Accessoires requis : un journal, des ciseaux et de la colle caoutchouc

Commencez par couper une fine lisière de papier journal d'environ 2.5cm (1 pouce) de largeur par 18cm (7 pouces) de longueur. Appliquez de la colle caoutchouc sur l'un des côtés de cette lisière et laissez sécher la colle. Durant votre spectacle, sortez la lisière de journal et pliez-la en deux (avec le côté collant vers l'intérieur). Coupez-la suivant l'axe du centre avec des ciseaux (ou des ciseaux de sécurité si vous êtes trop jeune). Dépliez lentement le papier journal. La colle fera en sorte que les 2 bouts de papier resterons collés et que la lisière semblera reconstituée.

117. ŒUF À CONFETTI

Accessoires requis : un œuf vide (instructions plus bas), des confettis (ou de petits bouts de papier que vous aurez découpés)

Demandez d'abord à un adulte de faire un trou (grosseur d'une pièce de 10 cents) dans le côté de l'œuf (pas le haut ou le bas) et videz-le. Vous aurez donc une coquille avec un trou (ne gaspillez pas l'œuf, faites-le cuire pour le petit déjeuner). Laissez la coquille sécher complètement. Une fois la coquille bien sèche, remplissez-la de confettis (vous pouvez acheter des confettis au magasin de costume ou couper plusieurs bouts de papier de soie). Collez ensuite un petit bout de papier sur le trou. Montrez l'œuf à vos spectateurs en cachant bien le trou. Pour le public, ceci n'est qu'un simple œuf. Écrasez rapidement l'œuf dans votre main et lancez-le dans les airs créant une pluie de confettis. Les morceaux de coquilles se mêleront aux confettis et l'œuf semble avoir disparu. NOTE* : ne jamais effectuer ce tour sur un plancher recouvert de tapis mais uniquement sur un plancher qui sera facile à balayer. Demandez toujours la permission de faire ce tour chez quelqu'un et ne jamais lancer les confettis vers les spectateurs. Lancez-les plutôt dans les airs.

118. LES ŒUFS TOUPIES

Accessoires requis : trois œufs crus et un œuf dur.

Deux ou trois œufs sont déposés sur la table alors que les spectateurs sont invités à essayer de faire tourner l'un d'eux tel une toupie. Il sera pratiquement impossible de réussir. L'œuf commence à tourner mais vacillera rapidement pour tomber sur le côté. Quand le magicien essaie, l'œuf tourne. La solution est simple : un des œufs est un œuf cuit dur mais cet œuf n'est pas sur la table au début. Après que plusieurs personnes ont effectuées des tentatives infructueuses, remplacement discrètement un des œufs par l'œuf dur. Cet œuf sera très facile à faire tourner.

119. COUP DE MAÎTRE

Accessoires requis : 10 jetons de dames rouges et un noir

Dix jetons sont empilés. Tous sont rouges sauf le quatrième du bas qui lui, est noir. Le magicien prend un autre jeton rouge et le dépose sur la tranche. En exerçant une pression, le jeton se dirige en direction de la pile. Plutôt que la pile s'effondre, le jeton noir se libère de la pile sans faire tomber le reste des jetons. Comme le jeton noir est à la hauteur parfaite pour recevoir l'impact du jeton rouge, il se délogera sans déranger les autres jetons.

120. LES JETONS MOBILES

Accessoires requis : sept jetons de dames, papier noir, ciseaux, ruban et morceau de papier

Une pile de jetons rouges est déposée sur la table avec un jeton noir au centre. La pile est couverte d'un tube de papier. Quand le tube est retiré, le jeton noir est maintenant au-dessous de la pile. Avant votre spectacle, découpez un bout de papier noir de la largeur d'un jeton. Entourez un jeton rouge de ce papier noir et collez-le en place. Tous les jetons sont donc rouges mais celui du centre comporte a l'aspect d'un jeton noir. Empilez les jetons de façon à ce que la pile ne soit pas parfaite. Le tube est utilisé pour redresser la pile. En redressant la pile, la boucle noire tombe à la base de la pile.

121. LA PILE QUI BOUGE

Accessoires requis : jetons de dames noirs et rouges, deux bouts de papier et de la peinture noire et rouge

Deux piles de jetons sont utilisées; une rouge et une noire. Un tube de papier est déposé autour de chaque pile et le haut est refermé pour bien cacher les jetons. La pile rouge doit placée loin de la pile noire. Le magicien annonce que les deux piles changeront de place. Lorsque les tubes sont retirés, les piles se sont effectivement déplacées. Vous devrez fabriquer deux jetons spéciaux. Le premier est un jeton rouge dont vous peindrez l'un des côtés en noir alors que le deuxième est un jeton noir avec un côté peinturé en rouge. Ces jetons sont les deux jetons qui se trouvent au bas de chaque pile. Lorsque la pile est recouverte du tube de papier, vous devez fermer le dessus et incliner la pile pour que l'on puisse voir le jeton du dessous. La pile noire semblera donc rouge, et vice-versa.

122. LES DÉS MAGNÉTIQUES

Accessoires requis : deux dés.

Deux dés sont déposés sur la table, un sur l'autre. Quand le dé supérieur est soulevé, le deuxième y reste attaché, comme s'il était magnétique. Placez le premier dé sur la table avec le « 1 » sur le dessus. Léchez le bout de votre doigt et appliquez la salive du côté « 1 » du dé supérieur. Quand les deux côtés « 1 » sont l'un contre l'autre, une succion se crée ils semblent donc être magnétiques.

123. LES DOMINOS

Accessoires requis : un ensemble de dominos.

Placez un ensemble de dominos sur la table et demandez à deux ou trois personnes d'aligner les dominos comme s'ils jouaient une partie. Juste avant que les spectateurs s'exécutent, écrivez quelque chose sur un bout de papier, pliez-le et déposez-le sur la table, à la vue de tous. À la fin de la partie, il y aura 2 rangées de dominos. Supposons que le chiffre à un bout est 5 et qu'à l'autre bout, c'est un 3. Quand le papier sera déplié, les chiffres 5 et 3 seront inscrits. Vous avez prédit le résultat! Avant votre spectacle, retirez l'un des dominos (pas un double). Les chiffres sur le domino retiré (dans ce cas-ci le 5 et le 3) seront à la fin de la série de dominos.

124. JE PEUX LIRE DANS VOS PENSÉES

Accessoire requis : un complice secret

Pour cette prochaine section, vous apprendrez des techniques de lecture de pensée similaires à celles utilisées dans Insaisissable 2. Un complice secret devra être présent, et vous devez avoir une confiance absolue en cette personne. Votre complice ne doit jamais dévoiler vos secrets. Pour la première démonstration, annoncez que vous aurez besoin d'un assistant. Vous choisirez bien entendu votre complice. Expliquez aux spectateurs que vous quitterez la pièce pendant que votre assistant choisira un objet au hasard. À votre retour, vous tenterez de deviner quel est cet objet. À votre retour, demandez à votre complice de pointer différents objets dans la pièce. Au préalable, vous vous serez entendus pour que le quatrième objet pointé soit le bon. N'arrêtez pas au quatrième objet, mais laisser le complice continuer à pointer pour évidemment l'interrompre en annonçant « Je l'ai » et confirmant à tous quel est l'objet choisi.

125. ENCORE SVP !

Accessoire requis : un complice secret

Si vous utilisez quelques fois l'effet précédent, certaines personnes pourraient en deviner le fonctionnement. Préparez donc un autre code avec votre assistant. La première fois, c'est le quatrième objet, la deuxième fois c'est le troisième objet, la troisième fois ce sera le sixième objet, etc. Si vous refaites ce stratagème trois ou quatre fois, les gens ne se douteront jamais de la méthode utilisée.

126. NOIR NOIR

Accessoire requis : Un assistant secret

Une autre variante du tour précédent est de demander à votre assistant secret de pointer quelque chose de noir juste avant de pointer le bon objet. Dès que vous voyez que votre assistant pointe quelque chose de noir, vous savez que le prochain objet sera le bon.

127. TRANSMISSION SILENCIEUSE 1 À 20

Accessoire requis : un complice secret

Vous annoncez que vous sortirez de la pièce et que tout le monde doit s'entendre pour choisir un chiffre entre 1 et 20. Choisissez votre assistant secret et dites : « Vous semblez être un bon transmetteur. Vous voulez participer ? ».

À votre retour, placez vos mains de chaque côté de sa tête en disant : « Ceci nous permet de communiquer ensemble ». Prétendez une concentration intense. Votre assistant doit contracter les muscles de sa mâchoire le nombre de fois équivalent au chiffre choisi. Vos mains camouflent le léger mouvement qui serait visible au niveau des tempes. Les spectateurs seront étonnés quand vous nommerez le chiffre choisi !

128. TRANSMISSION SILENCIEUSE DE 1 À 100

Accessoire requis : un complice secret

Vous pouvez également faire choisir un chiffre entre 1 et 100. Vous devrez tricher un peu car vous ne voulez certainement pas compter 85 mouvements de la mâchoire. Les premiers mouvements seront pour le premier chiffre (si le chiffre est 85, il ferait 8 mouvements de la mâchoire). Après les 8 coups, il prend une légère pause et fait 5 autres mouvements (pour le 5 de 85). Après beaucoup de pratique vous pouvez même donner le choix entre 1 et 1000. Vous serez capable, avec cette méthode, de rendre vos spectateurs fous et ce, même s'ils connaissaient la méthode de 1 à 20.

129. LA PRÉDICTION EN COULEUR

Accessoire requis : du papier et un crayon

Avant votre spectacle, écrivez sur 4 bouts de papier le nom de 4 couleurs différentes (vert, rouge, bleu et jaune). Pliez ces bouts de papier et déposez-les dans 4 poches différentes (en vous souvenant, de l'emplacement de chacune des couleurs). Prenez maintenant une feuille et écrivez les couleurs suivantes devant votre public : « noir, vert, rouge, bleu, jaune et blanc ». Dites : « oups ! J'avais oublié, le blanc et le noir ne sont pas réellement des couleurs ». Biffez ces couleurs de la liste et demandez à quelqu'un de choisir une des couleurs énumérées. Quand il nomme la couleur, prenez le papier dans votre poche, confirmant que vous aviez prédit la couleur choisie.

130. L'ENVELOPPE ET LA LECTURE DE PENSÉE

Accessoires requis : deux enveloppes, de la colle, du papier et un crayon

Voici une variante de l'effet précédent. Vous devrez confectionner une enveloppe spéciale. Collez d'abord deux enveloppes face à face de façon à ce qu'elles soient parfaitement alignées. Vous avez donc un rabat de chaque côté. Prenez un bout de papier et écrivez : « vous choisirez rouge ». De l'autre côté du même papier, écrivez : « vous choisirez jaune ». Déposez ce bout de papier dans une des deux enveloppes. Sur un autre bout de papier, écrivez « vous choisirez vert » et de l'autre côté, « vous choisirez bleu ». Déposez ce papier dans la seconde enveloppe. Déposez cette double-enveloppe dans votre poche. Demandez à un spectateur de nommer une couleur. Vous n'avez qu'à sortir l'enveloppe, ouvrir le bon côté et montrer le papier confirmant votre prédiction.

131. L'APPARITION DE LA CARTE DANS L'ENVELOPPE

Accessoires requis : deux enveloppes et une carte

En utilisant l'enveloppe spéciale du tour précédent, déposez un as de pique dans une des enveloppes et déposez-le tout dans votre poche. Au spectacle, dites à vos spectateurs que vous allez faire apparaitre magiquement un as de pique dans l'enveloppe. Montrez l'enveloppe vide et prétendez déposer un as invisible dans celle-ci. De façon discrète, retournez l'enveloppe au même moment que vous la déposez sur la table. Faites un geste magique au-dessus de l'enveloppe et affirmez « Je crois qu'il y a quelque chose dans l'enveloppe ». Ouvrez l'enveloppe et sortez la carte.

132. QU'Y-A-T-IL SUR LE PAPIER?

Accessoires requis : un bout de papier et un stylo

Le magicien demande à un spectateur d'écrire quelque chose sur un bout de papier, de le plier et de déposer le papier au sol. Pour s'assurer que le magicien ne peut rien voir, le spectateur est invité à mettre son pied sur le bout de papier. Le magicien dit ensuite que même s'il lui est impossible de voir ce qui est écrit, qu'il peut tout de même savoir ce qui est sur le papier. En fermant ses yeux, le magicien annonce : « votre pied ». Le spectateur ne peut être en désaccord.

133. LE TÉLÉPHONE PSYCHIQUE

Accessoires requis : un téléphone et un ami avec un téléphone

Le tour précédent peut également être effectué avec l'aide d'un complice qui a accès à un téléphone cellulaire. Informez-le qu'il recevra un appel d'une personne qui demandera à parler au GRAND RAMBINI. Quand il recevra l'appel, il doit simplement répondre : « le total des 3 dés est 21 ! ». Ce tour fonctionne à tout coup car votre complice saura toujours quoi répondre.

134. JE PRÉDIS !

Accessoires requis : un paquet de carte où la carte que vous désirez forcer est déjà placée sur le dessus, une tasse et 3 petits bouts de papier

Informez vos spectateurs que vous prédirez trois choses choisies. Demandez d'abord à un membre du public de couper le paquet de cartes. Vous allez effectuer le forçage en croix tout en laissant les paquets disposés en croix sans révéler la carte pour l'instant. Affirmez à votre public que vous allez inscrire votre prédiction sur bout de papier. En réalité, vous écrivez le nom de la carte que vous forcez. Déposez ce bout de papier dans la tasse. Demandez ensuite au spectateur de nommer un objet qui se trouve dans la pièce. Par exemple, supposons qu'il choisisse une chaise. Prenez donc un autre bout de papier en disant que vous allez y inscrire un chiffre au hasard. Évidemment, écrivez « chaise » sur ce bout de papier et déposez-le dans la tasse. Prenez finalement le dernier bout de papier et dites que vous y inscrirez la carte choisie par la coupe du spectateur. En réalité, vous écrivez le nombre que le spectateur vous a donné après avoir écrit la prédiction « chaise ». Déposez ce dernier bout de papier dans la tasse. Prenez le paquet et montrez la carte choisie et enfin versez le contenu de la tasse sur la table. Demandez au spectateur de lire vos prédictions. Tout le monde sera bien surpris de constater que vous avez réussi avec brio.

135. UN MESSAGE MAGIQUE

Accessoires requis : un sac de papier, un stylo et une dizaine de bouts de papier

Sur un bout de papier écrivez « l'objet choisi sera une chaise ». Déposez ce bout de papier dans votre poche. Demandez à vos spectateurs d'énumérer une liste d'objets domestiques et prétendez inscrire chacun d'eux sur les bouts de papier. En réalité, vous écrivez le mot « chaise » sur chacun en vous assurant que personne ne puisse vous voir. Faites une petite boule avec chaque bout de papier et déposez-les dans le sac. Secouez le sac et demandez à un spectateur de ne sortir qu'un seul bout de papier. Demandez au spectateur d'ouvrir le bout de papier et d'y lire le mot inscrit. Sortez maintenant la prédiction de votre poche. Non seulement un message est apparu, mais la prédiction s'avère exacte.

136. DES CHIFFRES !

Accessoires requis : un stylo et un bloc-notes

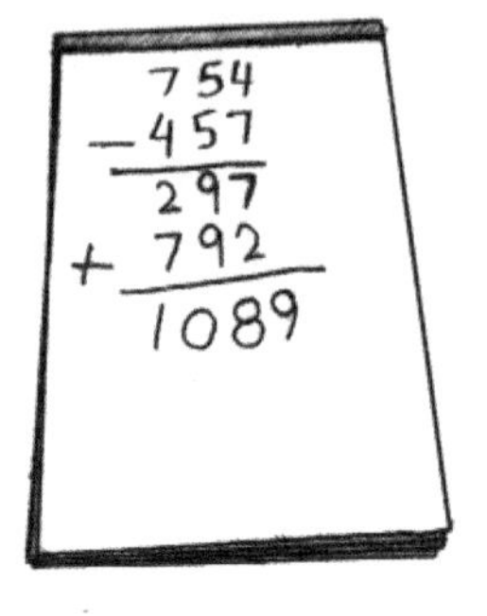

Sur un bout de papier, écrivez : « Le nombre sera 1089 ». Scellez ensuite votre prédiction dans une enveloppe. Produisez une feuille et un crayon en demandant : « Je voudrais que vous écriviez un nombre à 3 chiffres mais les 3 chiffres doivent être différents et le premier doit être plus élevé que le dernier ». Sous ce nombre, écrivez les mêmes chiffres mais à l'envers (donc si le nombre est 754 vous écrivez 457). Effectuez alors la soustraction des 2 nombres (vous pouvez utiliser une calculatrice si vous le désirez). Dans notre exemple, le résultat est 297. Inscrivez le résultat et, sous celui-ci, inscrivez encore une fois ce chiffre en ordre inverse (297 et 792). Annoncez : « Nous avons commencé avec un chiffre au hasard et nous l'avons grandement modifié. Il ne nous reste qu'à additionner ces 2 chiffres pour donner le résultat final ». Additionnez-les et vous obtiendrez toujours 1089 et ce, peu importe le chiffre de départ (si vous avez bien suivi les directives). Sortez l'enveloppe scellée et prouvez que la prédiction est exacte.

137. LE « BOOK TEST » 1089

Accessoires requis : un bloc-notes, un crayon et un livre comportant plus de 108 pages

Choisissez un livre de votre bibliothèque et ouvrez-le à la page 108. Trouvez le neuvième mot de la première ligne et inscrivez ce mot sur un bout de papier. Comme auparavant, déposez cette prédiction dans une enveloppe. En spectacle, suivez toutes les étapes du numéro « DES CHIFFRES » mais cette fois-ci, ne révélez pas le chiffre « 1089 » comme prédiction. Vous allez plutôt reprendre le livre que vous avez choisi et demander au spectateur de l'ouvrir à la page 108 et de lire le neuvième mot. À la lecture du mot, sortez votre prédiction et montrez-la à tous.

138. LES CRAYONS PSYCHIQUES

Accessoires requis : une boite de crayons ou de marqueurs

Montrez une boite de crayons et affirmez pouvoir deviner la couleur d'un crayon qui vous sera donné par un spectateur sans le voir. Tenez vos mains derrière vous et demandez à un spectateur de vous donner un crayon au hasard. Vous n'avez qu'à frotter légèrement le crayon sur votre ongle pour ensuite subtilement voir la couleur du crayon choisi.

139. L'HORLOGE MAGIQUE

Accessoires requis : une horloge ou une montre et un crayon (ou baguette magique)

Vous pouvez utiliser une montre ou d'une horloge pour deviner un numéro choisi par un spectateur. Demandez à l'un des spectateurs de penser à un nombre d'un à douze. Expliquez que vous allez taper avec votre doigt sur les chiffres de l'horloge. Commencez en disant qu'il doit commencer avec le chiffre auquel il pense en ajoutant un à chaque fois que vous tapez avec votre doigt. Par exemple, s'il pense au chiffre 9, il doit compter 10, 11, 12... et ce, à chaque fois que vous donnez un coup. Quand vous serez rendu à 20, demandez au spectateur de dire « stop ». Vous avez maintenant toutes les informations nécessaires pour révéler au spectateur le chiffre auquel il pensait. Pour les 7 premiers coups, vous pouvez taper sur n'importe quel chiffre du cadran de l'horloge. Mais sur le huitième, vous devez donner le coup sur le numéro 12. Vous continuerez par la suite dans le sens inverse des aiguilles d'une montre (ex : 11, 10, 9, 8...). Lorsque le spectateur vous dira d'arrêter, vous serez surpris de voir que votre doigt se trouve exactement sur son chiffre.

140. LE BRAS HYPNOTISÉ

Accessoire nécessaire : un membre du public

Demandez à un spectateur de se tenir dans l'embrasure d'une porte et dites-lui que vous allez hypnotiser ses bras. Dites-lui d'exercer une pression intense sur le cadre de porte avec ses deux bras (ses bras doivent longer le corps). Dites : « Je veux simplement vérifier que vous n'êtes pas capable de déplacer un mur car les bras qui peuvent déplacer un mur sont difficiles à hypnotiser ». Demandez-lui de continuer à pousser durant 45 secondes. Après ces 45 secondes, informez-le que ses bras sont maintenant hypnotisés et qu'ils lèveront d'eux-mêmes. Emmenez le spectateur hors de la porte. Sans pouvoir les retenir, les bras lèveront d'eux-mêmes !

141. LA JAMBE HYPNOTISÉE

Accessoire requis : un membre du public

Informez les spectateurs que vous comptez hypnotiser la jambe d'une personne du public et que vous en serez en contrôle. Affirmez au spectateur choisi que vous allez contrôler sa jambe pour qu'elle reproduise tout mouvement de la main de ce même spectateur. Demandez-lui de lever la jambe gauche et d'effectuer des cercles dans le sens des aiguilles d'une montre. Demandez-lui maintenant de faire des cercles avec le bras gauche mais cette fois, dans le sens inverse des aiguilles d'une montre. Montrez à tous que sa jambe fait maintenant des cercles dans le sens inverse également. Demandez-lui de nouveau de faire des cercles avec la jambe, dans le sens des aiguilles d'une montre, mais en immobilisant son bras. Demandez ensuite au spectateur d'allonger le bras gauche droit devant. La jambe gauche commencera à s'allonger de la même façon. Le secret de ce tour réside dans la science. Il est très difficile d'effectuer des mouvements différents avec les bras et les jambes en même temps; le cerveau tend donc à copier les mouvements du bras.

142. SECRETS RÉVÉLÉS

Accessoires requis : une feuille de papier pour imprimante coupée en quatre et quatre crayons.

Vous remarquerez que vos quatre bouts de papier (qui ont été déchirés d'une feuille complète) ont 2 cotés droits et 2 côtés déchirés. Gardez trois morceaux à l'écart car vous n'en avez besoin que d'un pour ce tour. Pendant votre spectacle, choisissez quatre spectateurs et informez-les que vous allez deviner leurs secrets. Déchirez le morceau de papier en quatre, donnez-en un à chaque personne en leur demandant d'y inscrire un secret. Reprenez les quatre morceaux de papiers (écriture face vers le bas). Vous pouvez même les mélanger. Lisez un à un les secrets. Vous serez facilement capable d'affirmer à qui appartient chaque secret. Comment ? Chaque bout de papier est unique; un bout aura deux côtés droits et deux côtés déchirés. Un autre aura trois côtés déchirés et un long côté droit. Un troisième aura trois côtés déchirés et un court côté droit. Le dernier aura 4 côtés déchirés. Vous n'avez qu'à mémoriser à quel spectateur appartient quel bout de papier.

143. ENCORE DE LA LECTURE DE PENSÉE

Accessoires requis : dix cartes, un crayon (ou baguette magique) et un complice

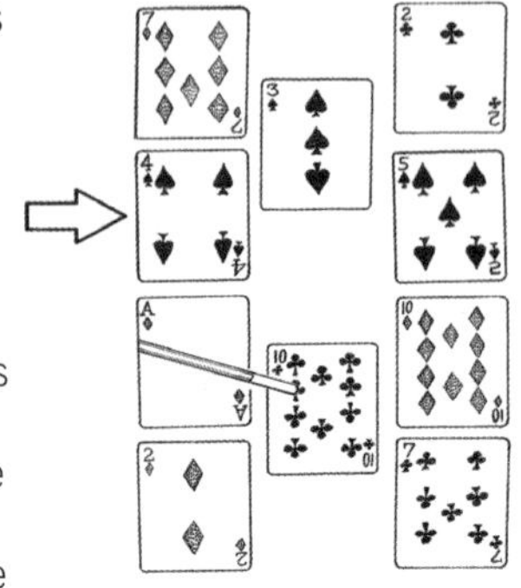

Dix cartes sont étalées sur la table et, alors que vous n'êtes pas dans la pièce, les spectateurs pensent à une seule de ces cartes. Vous demandez alors à une personne de taper une à une les cartes avec un crayon. Vous pourrez immédiatement connaître l'identité de la carte. Comment ? Les cartes sont disposées de la même façon que les symboles sur une carte de valeur « 10 » (deux colonnes de quatre et une colonne de deux placée entre les deux autres colonnes). Une des dix cartes doit être un 10 (par exemple le 10 de carreau). L'autre astuce est que l'assistant doit être votre complice. Lorsque venu le temps de taper sur le 10 de carreau, votre complice touchera le symbole sur la carte correspondant à l'emplacement de la carte choisie sur la table. Par exemple, si la carte choisie est la première de la deuxième colonne, l'assistant tapera le symbole carreau qui se trouve dans cette même position sur la carte. Ne révélez pas l'identité de la carte tout de suite, laissez-le terminer. Répétez ce truc aussi souvent que vous le voulez, la méthode est si incroyable que personne ne devinera comment il est effectué.

MAGIE DE RESTAURANT

144. DU SEL EN SUSPENSION !

Accessoires requis : une salière et un cure-dent

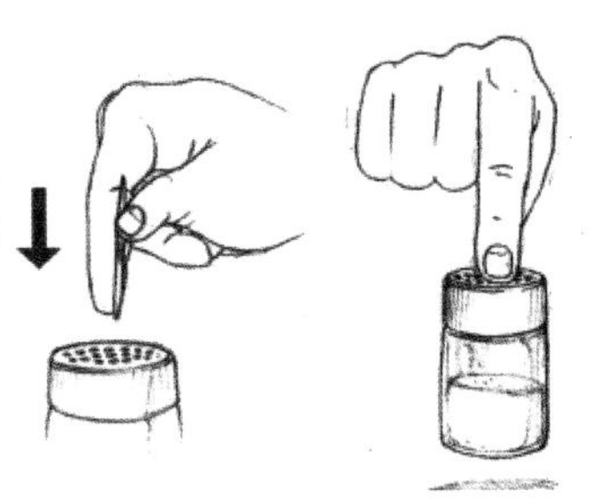

Dans ce tour, nous utiliserons un cure-dent comme accessoire magique. Procurez-vous une salière ou une poivrière. Dissimulez le cure-dents derrière votre index et tenez-le en place avec votre pouce. Maintenant, en allant toucher la salière avec votre index, poussez secrètement le cure-dent dans l'un des trous de la salière (comme l'illustration). Si vous levez maintenant votre main (avec l'index touchant toujours la salière), l'impression sera que la salière colle à vos doigts. En utilisant votre autre main, saisissez la salière et déposez-la sur la table. Laissez tomber secrètement le cure-dents par terre ou dans votre poche en disant : « J'ai vraiment une personnalité magnétique ! »

145. INCASSABLE !

Accessoires requis : deux cure-dents et une serviette de table

Pour cette illusion, munissez-vous d'une serviette de table et de deux cure-dents. Avant votre spectacle, disposez un cure-dent à l'intérieur de la couture de votre serviette de table. En performance, étalez la serviette de table et déposez l'autre cure-dent au centre. Pliez alors la serviette autour du cure-dent que vous allez alors donner l'impression de tenir. En réalité, vous allez tenir celui qui a été caché, laissant le second libre à l'intérieur. Demandez à un spectateur de casser le cure-dent à travers de la serviette. Demandez : « L'avez-vous senti briser ? » ou « L'avez-vous entendu briser ? ». Une fois la réponse, clamez : « alors ceci doit être de la vraie magie ! ». Dépliez la serviette et montrez le cure-dent intact.

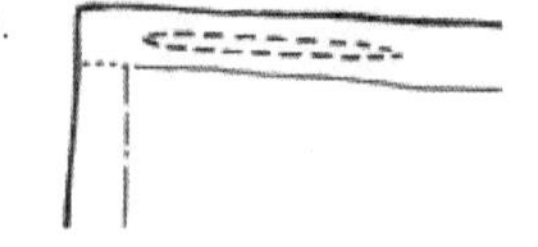

146. LE CURE-DENT CASSÉ ET RECONSTITUÉ

Accessoires requis : deux cure-dents

Tout d'abord, préparez le matériel requis pour cette illusion : cassez un cure-dent en deux. Pendant le spectacle, donnez un cure-dent intact pour vérification. Une fois la vérification terminée, tenez le cure-dent sur le bout des doigts de la main gauche. Avec un morceau cassé caché entre vos doigts de la main droite, amenez cette dernière au-dessus de la main gauche, couvrant partiellement le cure-dent pour un bref instant. Glissez la moitié du cure-dent de la main gauche sous vos doigts de sorte que seule la moitié du cure-dent soit encore visible. Prétendez casser ce cure-dent. Vous donnerez maintenant l'impression de montrer à tous le cure-dent cassé en montrant la moitié du cure-dent toujours dans votre main gauche ainsi que le morceau cassé de la main droite. Dites que vous avez besoin d'électricité statique pour réparer le tout. Montrez une fois de plus le morceau de la main droite et frottez le contre votre coude gauche en disant que vous récoltez ainsi l'électricité statique requise. Montrez la moitié de la main gauche et frottez-le contre votre coude droit. Ce faisant, placez votre main droite juste à côté de votre cou. Alors que vous frottez le cure-dent sur votre coudre droit, laissez tomber le morceau de la main droite à l'intérieur de votre chandail. Amenez les deux mains ensembles comme pour reconstituer les deux morceaux tout en glissant le cure-dent de la main gauche. Le cure-dent au complet sera maintenant bien en vue. Vous pouvez le redonner pour vérification.

147. LE CURE-DENT DE POCHE

Accessoires requis : deux cure-dents

Si vous désirez, vous pouvez préparer le tour précédent à l'avance pour maintenir vos mains libres pour effectuer d'autres tours. Insérez le demi cure-dent dans votre poche droite. Donnez le cure-dent complet pour vérification. Alors que le public vérifie le cure-dent, emparez-vous subtilement du cure-dent brisé dans votre poche droite. Effectuez le reste du tour tel que décrit au numéro précédent.

148. L'APPARITION ET DISPARITION DU CURE-DENT

Accessoires requis : un cure-dent et un bout de ruban adhésif

Avec le ruban, collez un cure-dent sur l'ongle de votre pouce avec la pointe du cure-dent vers la première phalange. Pour faire apparaitre le cure-dent, fermez le poing en pliant légèrement le pouce vers l'avant. Le cure-dent et l'ongle du pouce touchent donc à l'intérieur de votre index. Pour faire disparaitre le cure-dent, ouvrez votre main en pointant le pouce vers le haut. Assurez-vous de garder l'intérieur de votre pouce face aux spectateurs.

149. REGARDEZ OÙ VOUS LANCEZ

Accessoires requis : un cure-dent et un bout de ruban adhésif

Quand vous faites disparaitre le cure-dent, ne regardez pas votre pouce. Ce serait un indice sur l'endroit où se situe le cure-dent. Prétendez plutôt lancer le cure-dent. Si vous le faisiez vraiment, vous regarderiez dans cette direction donc suivez le cure-dent imaginaire de votre tête et vos yeux.

150. LE CURE-DENT TRISTE !

Accessoires requis : un cure-dent et un bout de serviette de papier mouillé

Pour ce tour, vous devez prétendre être en furie contre un cure-dent et ce dernier se mettra à pleurer. Avant votre spectacle, cachez un morceau de ouate (ou de serviette de papier) légèrement mouillée entre votre pouce et vos doigts. Prenez maintenant un cure-dent en le déposant comme sur l'illustration. Appliquez une légère pression sur la ouate laissant tomber quelques gouttes et dites : « je me suis fâché trop vite, le cure-dent pleure ». Laissez-le tomber sur la table alors que vous empochez la ouate. Terminez en disant : « on devrait toujours être gentil avec les cure-dents ».

151. LE CURE-DENT MAGNÉTIQUE

Accessoires requis : 2 cure-dents plats

Déposez un cure-dent plat (il ne doit pas être rond) sur la table et mettez en équilibre un second cure-dent sur le premier de façon à ce qu'aucun bout du second cure-dent ne touche la table. Affirmez aux spectateurs que le cure-dent est magnétique et que seul votre index peut le faire bouger. Amenez votre index légèrement à droite du cure-dent. Soufflez maintenant secrètement et légèrement du côté gauche du cure-dent. Le cure-dent semblera attiré vers votre doigt.

152. TOUT EST DANS LE COMPTAGE !

Accessoires requis : dix cure-dents et un crayon

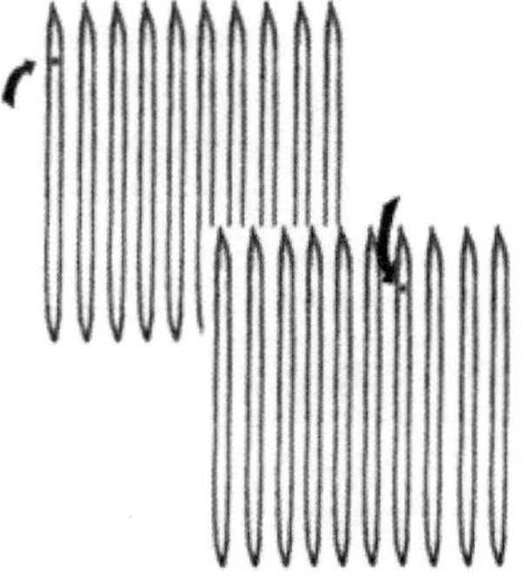

Sortez dix cure-dents et sur l'un d'eux, faites une petite indentation des deux côtés pour pourvoir le différencier facilement. Cette marque doit être la plus petite possible pour que vous soyez le seul à la voir. Pendant votre spectacle, disposez les dix cure-dents côte à côte. Assurez-vous que le cure-dent marqué soit complètement à gauche. Informez les spectateurs que vous allez vous retourner et que vous voudriez que l'un d'eux déplace entre un et dix cure-dent de la gauche vers la droite (un à un). Quand c'est fait, vous vous retournez et dites : « Incroyablement, je peux vous dire combien de cure-dents ont été déplacés ». Repérez le cure-dent marqué et comptez tous les cure-dents à sa droite, ainsi que celui-ci. Ce nombre sera le celui correspondant aux cure-dents déplacés par le spectateur. Une autre belle victoire

153. LE CURE-DENT QUI SAUTE

Accessoires requis : deux cure-dents

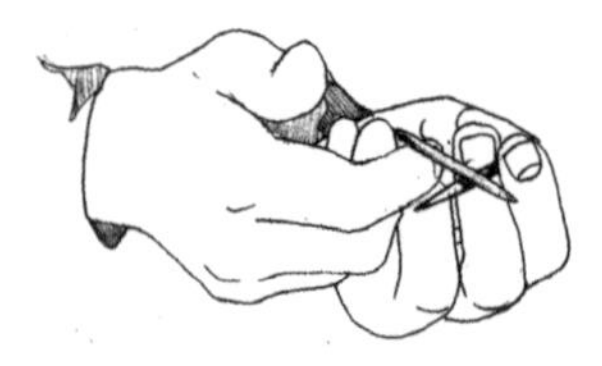

Voici un effet mystérieux qui rendra dingues vos amis qui essaieront d'expliquer ce qu'ils ont vu. Tenez le cure-dent comme sur l'illustration. Il est très important de le tenir exactement de cette façon ou l'illusion ne fonctionnera pas. Regardez particulièrement comment le cure-dent tient sur l'ongle de votre majeur. Mettez en équilibre un second cure-dent sur le dessus en le déposant entre l'index de l'autre main et le bout du premier cure-dent. Dites : « mon pouls magique est telle¬ment puissant qu'il peut parfois être visible ». Frottez lentement le premier cure-dent sur l'ongle du majeur. En faisant ceci très lentement, le cure-dent du dessus vacillera de haut en bas de façon étrange !

154. LA BANANE-KARATÉ

Accessoires requis : un cure dent et une banane

Avant votre spectacle, insérez le cure-dent au travers la pelure de la banane et utilisez ce point comme pivot pour couper le diamètre de la banane. Répétez à chaque deux centimètres de la banane. Pendant votre spectacle, sortez la banane et expliquez que vous préférez manger une banane coupée en morceaux. Prétendez donner des coups de karaté à la banane. Pelez maintenant votre banane en montrant qu'elle est coupée en tranches.

155. LA DISPARITION DU SUCRE

Accessoire requis : un sachet de sucre

Faites une petite incision sur le côté supérieur d'un sachet de sucre (faites-vous aider d'un adulte). Videz le contenu du sachet par cette incision. Remettez le sachet dans le contenant à sachets de sucre en gardant toujours à la vue où se trouve ce sachet. De plus, assurez-vous de garder l'incision vers vous pour éviter qu'elle ne soit détectée par le public. Au moment de faire ce tour, prenez le sachet et déchirez-le (pour l'ouvrir) là où vous avez fait l'incision. Fermez le poing gauche et, de votre main droite, prétendez vider le contenu du sachet. Assurez-vous qu'il n'y a aucun espace entre le sachet et votre poing pour éviter que les spectateurs constatent qu'aucun sucre n'en sort. Faites un geste magique et prétendez faire disparaitre le sucre. Ouvrez votre main pour montrer que le sucre a disparu.

156. CONVAINCANT

Accessoire requis : un sachet de sucre

Pour être encore plus convaincant, vous pourriez garder, pour le tour précédent, un peu de sucre dans le sachet. De cette façon, lorsque vous verserez le sucre dans votre poing, on le verra tomber. Ceci convaincra tout le monde que le sachet était bien plein.

157. SUCRÉ BON TOUR !

Accessoires requis : deux sachets de sucre

Vous pourriez faire le même tour avec un membre du public. Prenez d'abord votre sachet de sucre et demandez à un spectateur d'en prendre un également. Informez-le d'effectuer les mêmes gestes que vous. Faites disparaitre le sucre comme décrit plus haut. Évidemment le spectateur en sera incapable et se verra donc pris avec une main pleine de sucre.

158. LA FICELLE NON-COUPABLE

Accessoires nécessaires : une ficelle et des ciseaux

Pour ce tour, vous devrez vous munir d'une paille et d'un bout de ficelle plus longue que cette paille. Demandez à vos parents de faire une incision au centre de la paille (dans le sens de la longueur). Pendant votre spectacle, affirmez à tous cette paille est indestructible. Enfilez la ficelle dans la paille d'un bout à l'autre et pliez ensuite la

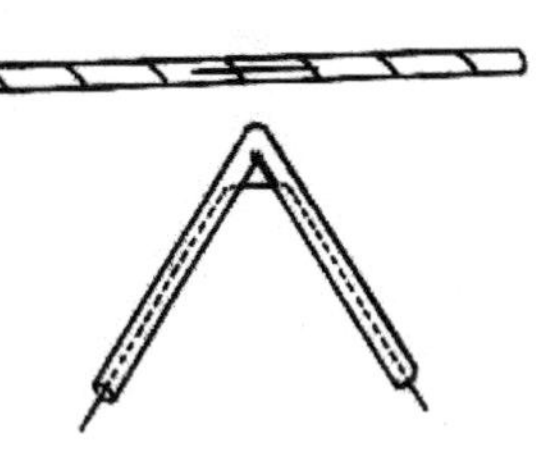

paille au centre. Assurez-vous que l'incision soit vers le bas et que personne ne peut la voir. Tirez maintenant les 2 bouts de la ficelle vers le bas, forçant la ficelle au travers de l'incision. Demandez à un spectateur de couper la paille au centre. Retirez maintenant les deux moitiés de paille et démontrez que la ficelle est complète. Non-coupable !.

159. LA PAILLE TÉLÉKINÉTIQUE

Accessoires requis : une paille et un verre

Saisissez une paille, retirez-la de son emballage et faites-la tenir en équilibre sur un verre. Approchez vos mains de la paille sans y toucher. Déplacez légèrement vos mains et la paille se mettra à bouger d'elle-même. Télékinésie ? Pas du tout. En retirant la paille de l'emballage, pincez celle-ci (pour l'écraser) entre le pouce et l'index. Ceci créera une charge d'électricité statique dans la paille. Cette électricité statique sera repoussée par celle dans votre corps, ce qui fera bouger la paille.

160. LE VERRE À TRAVERS LA TABLE

Accessoires requis : une pièce de monnaie, un verre et un napperon de papier (ou du papier journal)

Voici un tour idéal à effectuer au restaurant. Dites à vos amis que vous ferez passer une pièce de monnaie à travers la table. Déposez une pièce de monnaie sur la table et disposez par-dessus un verre avec l'ouverture vers le bas. Couvrez maintenant le verre avec votre napperon de papier (ou un papier journal). Assurez-vous que l'on voit bien la forme du verre à travers le napperon. Levez le tout pour montrer à tous que la pièce est encore là. En ce faisant, le verre doit être au-dessus de vos jambes. Alors que tous regardent la pièce de monnaie, laissez tomber le verre sur vos jambes en gardant intacte la forme du papier dans votre main. Grâce à cette forme, tous croiront que le verre est encore dans votre main. Replacez le napperon (toujours avec la forme du verre) au-dessus de la pièce de monnaie et frappez brusquement sur le tout pour aplatir complètement le napperon. Attendez un peu et sortez le verre d'en dessous de la table (en réalité sur vos jambes). Au début, nous vous suggérons de pratiquer avec un verre de plastique.

161. LE VERRE EN ÉQUILIBRE

Accessoires requis : un verre de plastique, deux cartes, des ciseaux et du ruban adhésif

Prenez deux cartes d'un paquet ordinaire (de préférence les jokers afin de préserver les cinquante-deux cartes de votre jeu) et coupez l'une d'entre elles dans le sens de la longueur. Puis, avec du ruban adhésif transparent, collez la tranche coupée de la demi-carte (le rabat) au centre du dos de la carte entière. Si vous avez réussi cette opération, votre carte ressemblera à un trépied lorsque le rabat est déplié, mais aura l'aspect d'une carte normale lorsque le rabat est replié. Pendant votre spectacle, sortez la carte truquée et posez-la à plat sur la table, avec le rabat en dessous. Personne ne doit voir le rabat ! Prenez ensuite un verre et affirmez à vos amis que, grâce à la magie, vous ferez tenir le verre en équilibre sur la carte ! Posez la carte verticalement sur la table et dépliez le rabat de façon à former un trépied (le rabat doit se trouver de votre côté bien sûr et non du côté du public). Posez le verre sur la tranche supérieure de la carte et du rabat. Lorsque vous écarterez vos mains, vous donnerez l'illusion que le verre est en équilibre sur une carte à jouer ordinaire ! Reprenez le verre et pliez rapidement le rabat derrière la carte avant de la poser à nouveau à plat sur la table.

162. SALÉ !

Accessoires requis : du sel, du poivre et un peigne

Sur une serviette de table, déposez du poivre de façon à former un petit tas. Ajoutez-y un peu de sel. Mélangez le tout et demandez à un spectateur combien de temps vous faudrait-il pour séparer le sel du poivre. Peu importe la réponse, dites que vous réussirez en moins de deux secondes. Pour effectuer ce tour, munissez-vous d'un peigne et peignez-vous les cheveux pendant quelques secondes. Emmenez rapidement le peigne au-dessus du poivre et du sel. Le sel s'agrippera automatiquement au peigne, laissant le poivre derrière.

163. LA PIÈCE DE MONNAIE DANS LE SACHET

Accessoires requis : un sachet de sucre et une pièce de monnaie empruntée

Comme dans le tour LA DISPARITION DU SUCRE, faites une incision mais cette fois-ci NE VIDEZ PAS le contenu du sachet. Insérez une pièce de monnaie dans l'ouverture. Déposez le sachet dans le contenant avec le reste des sachets, en vous assurant que l'ouverture soit vers le haut. Pendant votre performance, demandez une pièce de monnaie (de la même valeur que celle dans le sachet). Déposez la pièce sur la table devant vous. En prenant la pièce de votre main, faites-la glisser jusqu'à ce qu'elle tombe sur vos cuisses. Levez la main (prétendez que la pièce y est toujours) et prétendez la déposer dans votre main gauche. Faites un geste magique de votre main droite. Ouvrez la main gauche pour montrer que la pièce a disparue. Montrez les 2 mains, emparez-vous du sachet de sucre, ouvrez-le. Videz-le de son contenu pour montrer que la pièce est apparue dans le sachet.

164. LAISSEZ-LES OUVRIR LE SACHET

Accessoires requis : un sachet de sucre, une pièce de monnaie et un tube de colle

Pour ce tour, vous ouvrirez le sachet sur je joint (sur la couture, là où le sachet est collé, sur le rebord). Vous devrez pratiquer cette technique pour qu'elle soit à point. Choisissez un coin qui est facile à séparer. S'il n'y en a pas, pincez des deux côtés et tirez très légèrement pour que le sachet s'ouvre délicatement. Ne videz pas le contenu. Insérez la pièce à l'intérieur et recollez le sachet avec la colle. Vous pouvez maintenant donner le sachet et laisser le spectateur l'ouvrir.

165. LA PIÈCE DE MONNAIE SIGNÉE DANS LE SACHET

Accessoires requis : un sachet de sucre, une pièce de monnaie, un marqueur et un tube de colle

Voici une variante du tour PIÈCE DE MONNAIE DANS LE SACHET mais cette fois avec une pièce signée. Vos spectateurs ne pourront se douter de la présence d'un duplicata avec cette méthode. Faites la même préparation mais marquez la pièce de vos initiales avant de l'insérer et de recoller le tout. Durant votre spectacle, marquez une nouvelle pièce de vos initiales avant de la faire tomber sur vos cuisses. Continuez comme dans le tour précédent et faites ouvrir le sachet.

166. LE BILLET DE BANQUE DANS LE SACHET DE SUCRE

Accessoires requis : un sachet de sucre, un billet de banque et un tube de colle

Vous pouvez modifier le tour avec un billet de banque plutôt qu'une pièce de monnaie. Commencez par faire une incision dans le sachet comme dans le tour « LAISSEZ-LES OUVRIR LE SACHET ». Pliez un billet de banque de la façon suivante : pliez d'abord sur la largeur et repliez de nouveau. Le billet pourra maintenant entrer dans le sachet. Recollez les parois avec de la colle et déposez le sachet dans le contenant à sucre avec les autres sachets. Faites disparaitre le billet (une enveloppe à double-dos fonctionne bien, ou encore déposez-le billet dans votre poche). Faites ouvrir le sachet par un membre du public.

167. LA CARTE DANS LE SACHET DE SUCRE

Accessoires requis : un sachet de sucre, une carte et un tube de colle

Munissez-vous d'un paquet de carte et d'une carte duplicata. Par exemple, ce pourrait être le 5 de cœur. Pliez le 5 de cœur et insérez-le dans le sachet de sucre. Forcez un 5 de cœur et faites-le disparaitre (avec une enveloppe à double-dos). Faites ouvrir le sachet par un spectateur pour révéler la carte.

MAGIE AVEC DE L'ARGENT

168. LE JEU OÙ L'ON « PAIR »

Accessoires requis : une pièce chacune de 5 cents et 10 cents et cinq pièces de 1 cent.

Vous tenez des pièces dans votre main fermée et vous demandez à un spectateur s'il croit que l'argent dans la main représente un nombre pair ou impair. Le spectateur aura toujours tort ! Le stratagème fonctionnera toujours en utilisant une pièce chacune de 5 cents et de 10 cents, ainsi que cinq pièces de 1 cent. Si votre spectateur choisit « pair », ouvrez votre main et comptez les pièces : il y en a 7, un nombre impair. Si la personne choisit « impair », calculez le total de la valeur des pièces, qui est 20 cents (donc pair).

169. ANNÉE APRÈS ANNÉE

Accessoires requis : deux pièces de monnaie (dont une empruntée)

Vous devrez vous servir de votre mémoire pour ce tour, mais rien de trop compliqué. Vous n'aurez qu'à mémoriser 4 chiffres… une année pour être exact. En pratique, ce sera « 19 » ou « 20 » suivi de deux autres chiffres car les pièces de monnaies courantes sont toutes des années 1900 ou 2000. Prenez une pièce de 25 cents et mémorisez l'année. Cachez cette pièce dans votre main droite. Demandez une pièce équivalente à un spectateur. Déposez cette pièce sur la table devant vous. De votre main droite, faites subtilement glisser la pièce empruntée sur vos cuisses. Levez la main droite et fermez le poing. Affirmez au spectateur que vous tenterez de deviner l'année de la pièce. Un chiffre à la fois, vous révélez l'identité de l'année que vous avez mémorisé.

170. LA REINE QUI PLEURE

Accessoires requis : une pièce de monnaie et une serviette de papier mouillée

Vous pourriez faire la même chose avec une autre pièce de monnaie. Cachez un morceau de ouate (ou de serviette de papier) mouillé derrière la pièce d'un dollar. Expliquez que vous serrerez la pièce si fort que la reine se mettra à pleurer. Comme dans un effet précédent, appliquez une pression sur la ouate et l'eau coulera comme des larmes le long de la pièce.

171. LA TÊTE À L'ENVERS

Accessoires requis : un billet de banque

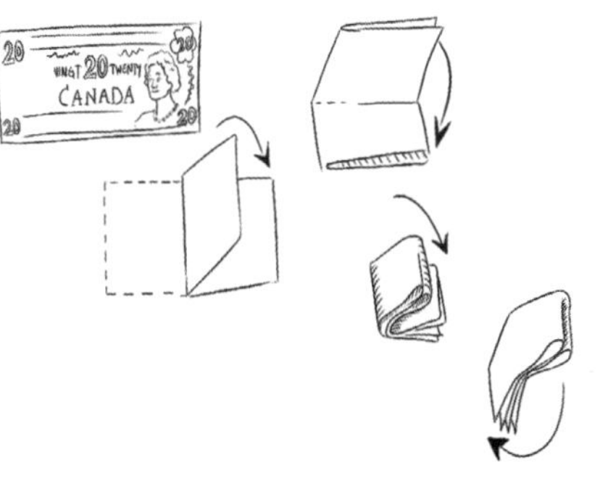

1. Empruntez un billet de banque (20 $ par exemple), en rassurant le spectateur que vous lui retournerez. Tenez le billet de façon à ce que la tête de la Reine Élizabeth soit face aux spectateurs.
2. Pliez le billet en deux de gauche à droite.
3. Maintenant en 4, de haut en bas vers vous.
4. Pliez-le une dernière fois de gauche à droite. Dites : « tout ce pliage doit rendre la Reine étourdie ».
5. Dépliez la partie du bas vers la gauche et dépliez ensuite le reste de la même façon que vous l'avez plié mais à l'inverse. La Reine aura maintenant la tête à l'envers. En terminant dites : « elle la tête à l'envers car elle ne comprend pas comment j'ai fait ! ».

172. L'APPARITION DE LA PIÈCE

Accessoires requis : une pièce de monnaie, un verre d'eau et une soucoupe

Déposez un 25 cents sur la table et posez un verre d'eau par-dessus. Déposez une soucoupe sur le verre. Demandez au spectateur de confirmer ce que le verre contient. « De l'eau bien sûr ». Demandez ensuite ce qui se trouve SOUS le verre. Rien ! Levez la soucoupe et le verre pour montrer qu'il y a une pièce. Essayez, vous verrez !

173. LE TOURNI-PIÈCE FRICTION

Accessoires requis : une pièce de monnaie et vos doigts

Affirmez aux spectateurs qu'il vous est possible de faire tournoyer une pièce de monnaie grâce à la friction. Tenez une pièce de 1$ ou 2$ à la verticale contre la table avec votre index droit. De votre index gauche, venez frotter votre index droit. Frappez secrètement la pièce de monnaie de votre pouce gauche et au même moment, enlevez votre index droit. La pièce de monnaie tournera sur la table.

174. LA PIÈCE BOUCHONNÉE

Accessoires requis : trois bouchons de liège, une pièce de monnaie, du fil à pêche, de la colle ou du ruban.

Avant votre spectacle, collez un petit bout de fil à pêche à une pièce de monnaie de façon à ce que 2 cm dépassent de la pièce. Comme le fil à pêche est presque invisible, vous serez la seule personne à le voir. Pendant votre spectacle, sortez la pièce et les trois bouchons. Demandez à un spectateur de mettre un des bouchons par-dessus la pièce et de déposer les 2 autre bouchons sur la table. Demandez-lui maintenant de mélanger les 3 bouchons alors que votre regard est tourné. Quand vous êtes prêts, vous pourrez immédiatement où se trouve la pièce grâce au bout de fil à pêche.

175. COUPÉ EN MORCEAUX

Accessoires requis : trois enveloppes, une paire de ciseaux et deux bouts de papier de la grandeur d'un billet de banque.

Faites une marque secrète au dos d'une des enveloppes avec un stylo. Assurez-vous que cette marque vous soit visible d'un coup d'œil rapide; vous pourrez la voir sans que votre public l'aperçoive. Pendant votre spectacle, sortez les trois enveloppes et les deux bouts de papier. Empruntez un billet de manque. Pliez les bouts de papier et le billet de banque en quatre. Insérez le billet de banque dans l'enveloppe marquée alors que vous insérez les deux bouts de papier dans les autres enveloppes. Scellez toutes les enveloppes et demandez à un spectateur de les mélanger. Reprenez les enveloppes une à la fois. Si la première n'a pas de marque, prenez les ciseaux et coupez-la en petits morceaux (si vous êtes trop jeune pour utiliser les ciseaux, demandez à un adulte de couper). Si l'enveloppe possède la marque, mettez-là de côté. Prenez la seconde enveloppe; si elle ne comporte toujours pas de marque, coupez-la également en petits morceaux. Si l'enveloppe a la marque, mettez-la de côté. Prenez la dernière enveloppe et répétez les étapes précédentes. Au final, deux enveloppes auront été réduites en miettes et une sera intacte. Donnez l'enveloppe au spectateur pour qu'il puisse reprendre son billet.

176. LA PIÈCE EN ÉQUILIBRE

Accessoires requis : une pièce et un nouveau billet de banque !

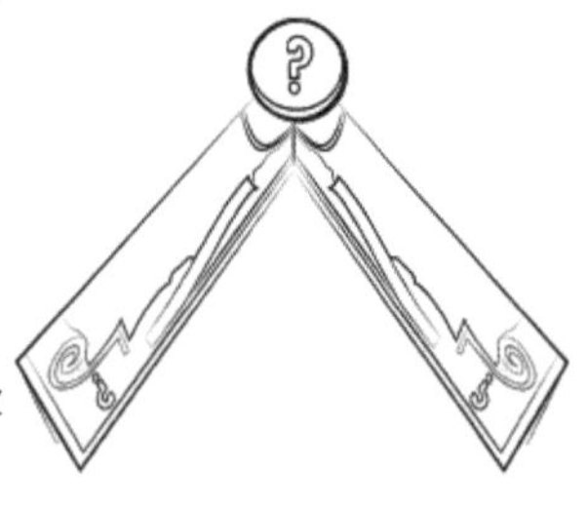

Pliez le billet (qui doit être le plus neuf possible) en 2 de haut en bas. Repliez-le mais cette fois-ci d'un côté à l'autre. Déposez-le sur la table avec l'ouverture vers le bas de façon à lui donner la forme d'un « V ». Placez votre pièce de monnaie (idéalement une pièce de 25 cents) au milieu du « V ». Prenez les deux bouts du billet et commencez à les déplier. La pièce restera en équilibre au centre même si le billet est presque droit.

177. LA PIÈCE PARLANTE

Accessoires requis : une pièce de monnaie, un petit bout de ruban adhésif, et un long bout de fil à pêche ou fil noir.

Avec l'éclairage ambiant tamisé, une pièce est déposée dans un verre de vitre. La pièce se met à bouger seule en sautant dans le verre. Vous énoncez qu'un seul saut de la pièce voudra dire « oui » alors que deux sauts signifient « non ». Après avoir répondu à plusieurs questions, la pièce saute hors du verre. Tout votre matériel pourra être vérifié par un spectateur. Avant le spectacle, attachez un long bout de ficelle noir à la pièce avec du ruban. Tenez l'autre bout de la ficelle sous la table. Chaque fois que vous tirez sur la ficelle, la pièce saute. À la fin, tirez très vigoureusement. La pièce sera donc libre du fil noir et bondira hors du verre.

178. LA PIÈCE QUI DISPARAIT DANS LE FOULARD

Accessoires requis : une pièce de monnaie et un foulard

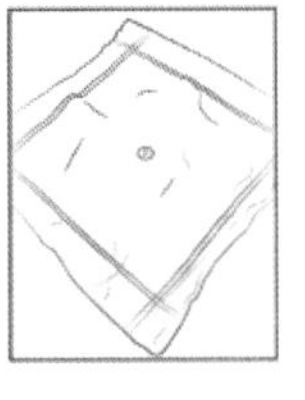

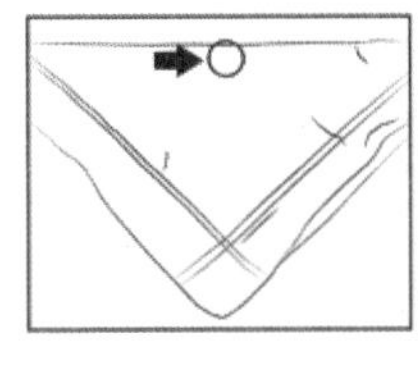

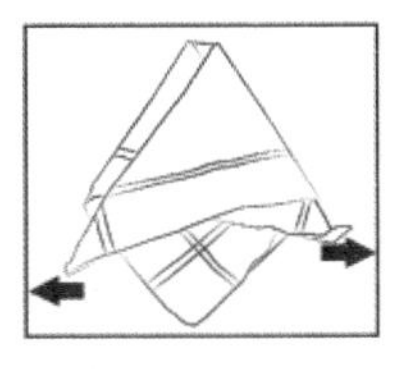

Disposez un foulard sur la table et déposez une pièce au centre. Pliez le foulard d'un coin à l'autre et par-dessus la pièce de monnaie. Prenez le coin droit et pliez-le diagonalement comme sur la photo. Faites la même chose avec le coin de gauche. Agrippez les 2 coins et tirez vers l'extérieur. Ceci créera une pochette qui va empêchera la pièce de tomber. La pièce semble avoir disparue.

179. DE PAPIER À ARGENT

Accessoires requis : un billet de banque, un morceau de papier de la grosseur d'un billet et un tube de colle.

Pliez le papier et le billet en 8 : en deux de côté à côté, encore en deux de côté à côté et en deux mais cette fois de haut en bas. Dépliez le billet et le papier et collez le coin inférieur gauche du billet sur même coin du papier. Repliez le billet et vous constaterez la création d'un petit paquet au bas du papier. Pendant votre spectacle, sortez le papier avec le billet face à vous et caché dans votre main. Pliez le papier comme précédemment. Tournez maintenant le paquet de sorte que le billet soit face aux spectateurs. Dépliez le billet en gardant le papier vers vous et caché dans votre main. Le papier semble s'être transformé en billet de banque.

180. ARGENT MULTIPLIANT

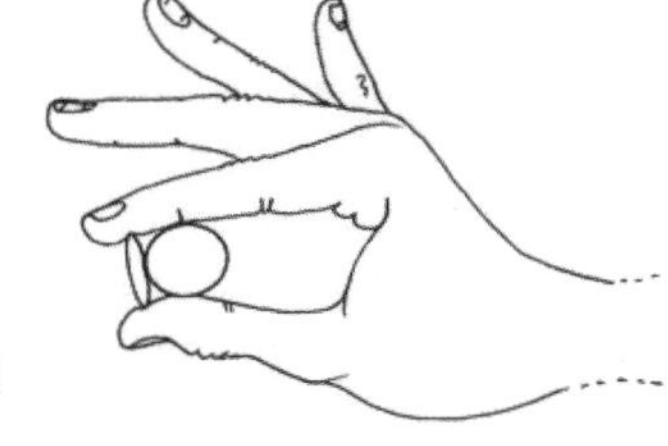

Accessoires requis : deux pièces de 25 cents et une pièce de 5 cents

Tenez d'abord les deux pièces de 25 cents face vers le haut entre votre index et votre pouce. Tenez la pièce de 5 cents, face vers l'avant, entre votre pouce et index devant les pièces de 25 cents. Vos doigts camouflent l'épaisseur des 25 cents par les côtés alors que le 5 cents en cache le devant. En spectacle, montrez la pièce de 5 cents. Assurez-vous de ne montrer que le 5 cents. Montrez votre autre main vide et fermez cette main autour des trois pièces. Ouvrez maintenant votre main en montrant que vous avez maintenant trois pièces dont les deux 25 cents bien trop gros pour avoir été cachés.

181. LA DISPARITION À L'EMPALMAGE DES DOIGTS

Accessoires requis : une grande pièce de monnaiee

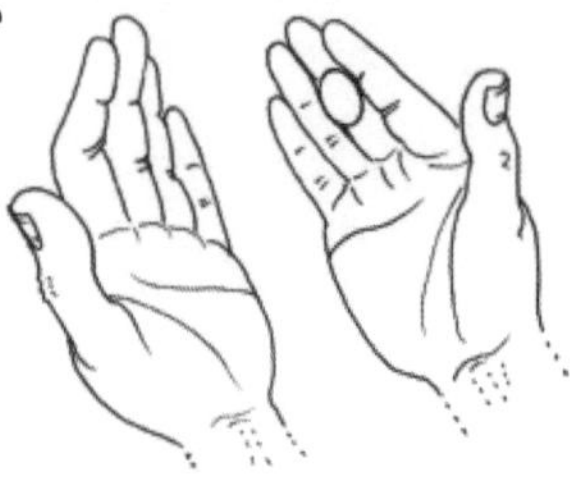

Ce tour est une façon classique de faire disparaitre une pièce. Prenez un 25 cents, et laissez-le tomber sur vos doigts de la main droite. Gardez la pièce sur le majeur tout en exerçant une pression sur la pièce avec l'index et l'annulaire. La pièce restera en place. Prétendez que vous mettez la pièce dans la main gauche en tournant votre main droite. Fermez rapidement la main gauche avant de bouger la main droite à nouveau. Prétendez prendre de la poussière magique dans votre poche avec votre main droite. Laissez-y la pièce. Ressortez la main droite et prétendez déposer la poussière magique sur votre main gauche. Ouvrez lentement la main gauche pour montrer que la pièce a disparu.

182. LA PIÈCE DERRIÈRE L'OREILLE

Accessoires requis : une pièce de monnaie et un spectateur...avec des oreilles !

Un classique de la magie est de faire disparaitre une pièce et de la faire réapparaitre derrière l'oreille d'un spectateur. Commencez par faire disparaitre la pièce en utilisant la technique d'empalmage des doigts comme au numéro précédent mais omettez la poussière magique. Portez votre main derrière l'oreille d'un spectateur et sortez-en la pièce. Tout le monde sera épaté. Vous pouvez également la faire apparaître des airs ou de tout autre endroit.

183. LA PIÈCE SIGNÉE DANS L'ORANGE

Accessoires requis : une petite pièce de monnaie, un marqueur, un couteau (pas trop acéré), un morceau de cire et une orange.

Avant votre spectacle, collez un bout de cire (comme dans les bouteilles en bonbon) sur le côté d'un couteau. Pendant votre spectacle, sortez le couteau, l'orange, le marqueur et la pièce de monnaie. Faites signer cette pièce. Faites disparaitre la pièce en empalmage des doigts tel que décrit plus haut. Alors que vous montrez que votre main gauche est vide, collez la pièce au bout de cire sur le couteau alors que vous prenez celui-ci. Gardez ce côté du couteau face à vous. Saisissez l'orange de votre main gauche et commencez à la couper. Alors que vous avez coupé la moitié de l'orange, exercez une légère pression sur celle-ci de façon à maintenir la pièce à l'intérieur l'orange. Une fois l'orange coupée au complet, séparez les deux parties d'orange et montrez que la pièce signée est à l'intérieur.

184. LA BANANO-CARTE

Accessoires requis : une banane, un cure-dent et un paquet de cartes.

La veille d'un spectacle, inscrivez le nom d'une carte sur la banane au moyen d'un cure-dent. N'appuyez pas trop fort – utilisez la même pression qu'avec un stylo sur une feuille. Le lendemain, cette inscription aura brunie. Pendant votre spectacle, forcez la carte et expliquez que vous êtes incapable de la trouver. Affirmez que le potassium est excellent pour la mémoire. Demandez au spectateur de vous donner la banane. Imaginez la réaction de tous et chacun lorsque le nom de la carte est inscrit sur la banane.

185. LA PIÈCE QUI DISPARAIT

Accessoires requis : une pièce de monnaie, un foulard et un complice

Vous devrez avoir recours à votre assistant secret pour ce tour. Placez une pièce de monnaie sur votre main et couvrez le tout avec un foulard. Promenez-vous parmi les spectateurs et demandez à tous et chacun de légèrement soulever le foulard afin de s'assurer que la pièce est toujours là. Votre assistant secret sera la dernière personne à soulever le foulard, et il devra discrètement prendre la pièce. Revenez à l'avant de la salle et retirez le foulard pour montrer que la pièce a disparu.

186. LA TASSE À MONNAIE PSYCHIQUE

Accessoires requis : quatre pièces de monnaie différentes et un complice

Encore une fois, votre assistant secret devra être présent pour ce tour. Déposez sur la table une tasse munie d'une anse et sortez quatre pièces de monnaie, une chacune de 1 cent, 5 cents, 10 cents et 25 cents. Quittez la pièce en expliquant aux spectateurs qu'ils doivent choisir une pièce. Votre assistant doit maintenant couvrir la pièce choisie et cacher les autres pièces. Ce que tous ignorent est que votre assistant oriente l'anse de la tasse vers la valeur de la pièce choisie. Imaginez que votre tasse est une horloge. Votre assistant n'a qu'à orienter l'anse vers le 12 pour le 25 cents, vers le 3 pour la pièce de 10 sous, vers le 6 pour le 5 sous et finalement vers le 9 pour la pièce de 1 cent. Revenez dans la salle et selon la position de la poignée, révélez la pièce cachée sous la tasse.

187. LA DISPARITION DE LA PIÈCE DE LA BOITE D'ALLUMETTES

Accessoires requis : une boite d'allumettes et une pièce de monnaie

Une pièce est déposée dans une boite d'allumettes et celle-ci est secouée pour prouver que la pièce s'y trouve toujours. Lorsque la boite est ouverte à nouveau, la pièce a disparue. Ce tour est possible grâce à une petite incision à un bout de la boite (tout juste assez grande pour permettre à la pièce d'y passer). Cette ouverture ne sera pas remarquée par les spectateurs. Quand vous secouez la boite, on peut bien entendre la pièce, mais dès que vous inclinez la boite vers vous, la pièce en sortira. De l'autre main, saisissez la boite et déposez-la en l'ouvrant, alors que vous déposez la pièce dans votre poche.

188. LA PIÈCE SUPPLÉMENTAIRE

Accessoires requis : quatre pièces de monnaie et du ruban adhésif collant des 2 côtés.

Trois pièces sont étalées sur la table. Les 2 mains sont montrées vides. Votre main droite balaie les pièces dans la main gauche. Quand la main gauche est ouverte, il y a maintenant 4 pièces. Avant votre spectacle, collez une pièce sur le côté de la table. Alors que la main gauche attrape les pièces, utilisez les doigts de la main gauche pour 'voler' la pièce. Laissez tomber cette pièce dans la main avec les autres.

189. LA PIÈCE ATOMIQUE

Accessoires nécessaires : une pièce de monnaie et du ruban adhésif à double face

Expliquez au public que vous frotterez une pièce avec tant de vigueur qu'elle se dissoudra. Avant votre spectacle, collez un bout de ruban sous la pièce. Déposez la pièce sur votre main gauche et couvrez votre main gauche de votre main droite en forme de croix. Alors que vous faites ce geste, déplacez la pièce de la paume au dos de la main gauche, avec le bout des doigts de la main droite. Comme la pièce est cachée sur la main gauche montrez vos deux paumes. Pour faire réapparaître la pièce, frottez vos mains ensemble alors que la main droite va chercher la pièce.

190. LA PÉNÉTRATION DE LA PIÈCE

Accessoires requis : cinq pièces de monnaie et du ruban adhésif à double face.

Quatre pièces sont étalées sur la table. Prenez une pièce avec la main gauche et emmenez-la sous la table. Couvrez les trois autres pièces avec la main droite. Vous ressortez la main gauche et laissez tomber 2 pièces sur la table alors qu'en levant la main droite, il ne reste que 2 pièces. Très simple : une autre pièce est utilisée. Cette dernière est collée sous la table avec le ruban. Lorsque votre main est sous la table, prenez simplement la pièce. Pour faire disparaitre une des pièces sous la main droite, collez un petit bout de ruban sur une pièce. Quand vous levez la main, la pièce reste collée à votre paume. Astucieux !

191. LE DÉTECTEUR INTELLIGENT

Accessoires requis : une grande pièce de monnaie et un spectateur crédule

Cette blague classique fera assurément rire votre public ! Appuyez une pièce de monnaie sur votre front pendant à peu près 10 secondes, jusqu'à ce qu'elle y colle. Tenez maintenant votre main droite sous votre front alors que votre main gauche frappe légèrement le derrière de votre tête à répétition, jusqu'à ce que la pièce tombe dans votre main. Expliquez que ce tour est un détecteur d'intelligence – plus le nombre de coups requis pour faire tomber la pièce est élevé, plus vous êtes intelligent. Appuyez la pièce contre le front d'un spectateur pendant 10 secondes. Retirez la pièce et garder la dans votre main. Comme vous avez appuyé assez longtemps, le spectateur croira toujours avoir la pièce au front. Le public rigolera en voyant le spectateur se frapper la tête sans arrêt, croyant à son intelligence supérieure !

192. LA PILE OU FACE ?

Accessoires requis : une pièce de monnaie et de la pratique !

Dans votre main droite, déposez une pièce avec la face vers le haut. Tapez le dos de votre main droite avec la pièce comme on le ferait pour jouer à pile ou face. Évidemment la pièce est maintenant du côté pile. Il est par contre possible de faire demeurer la pièce du côté face. C'est même un effet indétectable. En donnant une petite torsion, la pièce pivotera et seule la main changera de côté. Pratiquez plusieurs fois pour parfaire votre synchronisation.

193. LA PIÈCE DANS LE NŒUD

Accessoires requis : une pièce de monnaie et un foulard

Un foulard est tordu tel une corde. Un nœud est noué au centre et le tout donné à un membre du public. Le magicien fait disparaitre une pièce de monnaie. Lorsque le nœud dans le foulard est dénoué, la pièce s'y trouve. La pièce disparait grâce à l'empalmage des doigts de la main droite. Quand vous tortillonnez le foulard, un « tube » est créé tout le long. Vous n'avez qu'à faire glisser la pièce dans l'ouverture. La pièce se logera au centre, où le nœud se situe.

194. PIÈCE SIGNÉE DANS LE NŒUD

Accessoires requis : une pièce de monnaie, un foulard et un marqueur indélébile

Comme il n'y a qu'une pièce utilisée dans le tour précédent, il vous est possible de répéter le tour tout en augmentant l'effet. Faites signer la pièce. Le spectateur pourrait aussi y faire un dessin. Faites disparaitre la pièce. L'auditoire sera étonné de voir la pièce signée dans le foulard. e dans le foulard.

195. LA DOUBLE DISPARITION DU FOULARD

Accessoires requis : deux pièces de monnaie et deux foulards

En combinant les tours #179 et #194, vous pouvez développer une routine extraordinaire. Tout comme dans le tour LA PIÈCE QUI DISPARAIT DANS LE FOULARD, faites disparaitre une pièce de monnaie et ensuite, comme vous l'avez appris dans le tour PIÈCE DANS LE NŒUD, faites apparaître un duplicata dans un foulard avec un nœud. Ce type de tour est appelé une transposition – où un objet disparait d'un endroit et apparait ailleurs.

196. UNE AUTRE DISPARITION DU FOULARD

Accessoires requis : un foulard, une pièce de monnaie et un élastique

Une pièce de monnaie est poussée dans le centre d'un foulard. Quand le foulard est secoué, la pièce a disparue. Étirez un élastique entre le pouce et l'index et tenez cette main sous le centre du foulard. Quand vous poussez la pièce, vous la passez à travers du centre de l'élastique. Relâchez maintenant l'élastique. Celui-ci formera une pochette qui maintiendra la pièce en place. Même en secouant le foulard, la pièce restera introuvable.

197. TOC-TOC PIÈCE

Accessoire requis: une pièce de monnaie

Ce tour devrait être effectué sur une table de bois. Le magicien lance une pièce d'une main à l'autre. Il tend son bras et dit : « prenez la pièce » tout en se servant de la pièce pour faire un « toc » sur la table. Lorsque le spectateur tente de prendre la pièce, celle-ci a disparu. La solution est simple. La dernière fois que vous lancez la pièce de la main gauche à la main droite, vous ne faites que prétendre la lancer et vous prétendez aussi l'attraper de la main droite alors que votre main gauche va sous la table. Alors que vous semblez déposer la pièce sur la table, vous faites un « toc » avec la pièce sous la table. Grâce à ce son, la pièce semble toujours être dans votre main droite.

198. LA PIÈCE PARLANTE

Accessoires requis : une pièce de monnaie, un petit bout de ruban adhésif, et un long bout de fil à pêche ou fil noir.

Avec l'éclairage ambiant tamisé, une pièce est déposée dans un verre de vitre. La pièce se met à bouger seule en sautant dans le verre. Vous énoncez qu'un seul saut de la pièce voudra dire « oui » alors que deux sauts signifient « non ». Après avoir répondu à plusieurs questions, la pièce saute hors du verre. Tout votre matériel pourra être vérifié par un spectateur. Avant le spectacle, attachez un long bout de ficelle noir à la pièce avec du ruban. Tenez l'autre bout de la ficelle sous la table. Chaque fois que vous tirez sur la ficelle, la pièce saute. À la fin, tirez très vigoureusement. La pièce sera donc libre du fil noir et bondira hors du verre.

199. LA PIÈCE OBÉISSANTE

Accessoires requis : deux pièces de 5 cents, une de 10 cents, un verre et une table recouverte d'une nappe.

Un verre est déposé ouverture vers le bas sur deux pièces de 5 cents. Le verre doit être en équilibre sur les deux pièces (une pièce de chaque côté). Une pièce de 10 cents est envoyée sous le verre, entre les deux 5 cents. Vous expliquez que vous réussirez à faire sortir la pièce de 10 cents. Vous réussirez ce tour en « grattant » la nappe à répétition très près du verre. La pièce sortira d'elle-même.

200. LA PIÈCE QUI VOYAGE

Accessoires requis : deux pièces de monnaie identiques et un pantalon avec revers

Le magicien emprunte une pièce de monnaie et la dépose sous son soulier gauche. Quand il lève son pied à nouveau, la pièce a disparu et est maintenant sous le soulier droit. Ce tour devrait être fait lorsqu'assis. Mettez une pièce secrètement sous votre soulier droit. Lorsque vous empruntez la pièce, prétendez la déposer sous votre pied gauche alors qu'en réalité, vous laissez tomber la pièce dans le revers de votre pantalon. Simple mais efficace. Soulevez les 2 pieds pour montrer la transposition.

201. PIÈCE À TRAVERS LA SERVIETTE DE TABLE

Accessoires requis : un foulard et une pièce de monnaie

Tenez une pièce de monnaie entre votre index et votre pouce et couvrez le toutd'une serviette de table. Agrippez la serviette avec votre pouce tel qu'illustré.Prenez le bout de la serviette qui se trouve à l'avant et tirez-le pour révéler la pièce. Secouez vigoureusement la serviette vers l'avant de sorte que les deuxbouts de la serviette glissent par-dessus la pièce. Il semble que vous n'avez quetiré un bout de la serviette pour prouver que la pièce s'y trouve toujours mais en réalité, la pièce est maintenant libre et cachée derrière. Tordez la serviette sous la pièce jusqu'à ce que cette torsion fasse sortir la pièce et que celle-ci sorte complètement de la serviette de table. La pièce semble passer au travers de la serviette. Tout le matériel utilisé peut être donné aux spectateurs pour vérification.

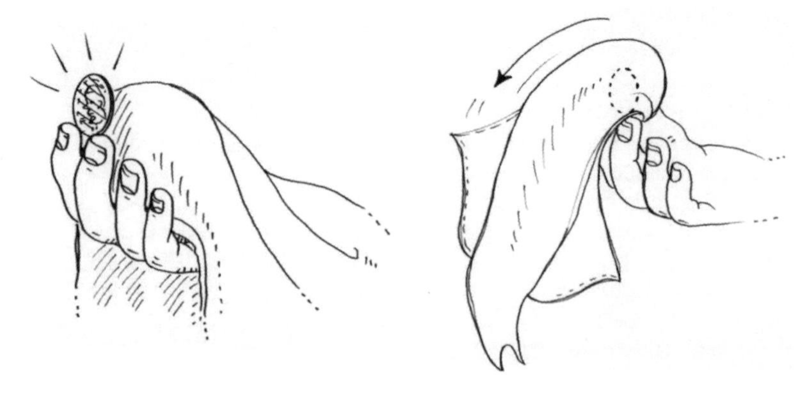